JB JOSSEY-BASS™
A Wiley Brand

87 Ways to Make Your Website More Volunteer-Friendly

Scott C. Stevenson, Editor

WILEY

87 Ways to Make Your Website More Volunteer Friendly

Published by

Stevenson, Inc.

P.O. Box 4528 • Sioux City, Iowa • 51104
Phone 712.239.3010 • Fax 712.239.2166

www.stevensoninc.com

TABLE OF CONTENTS

TABLE OF CONTENTS

87 Ways to Make Your Website More Volunteer Friendly

1. Three Ways to Recruit Volunteers Online

Have you ever considered using the Web to recruit volunteers? Following is a list of ways to utilize the Internet to increase your volunteer numbers.

1. **Use an online opportunities list.** Do you include a detailed position description? The more information you can give the better. Attention spans are short; give the surfer as much information as possible, right from the beginning. Also include your e-mail address or create a separate e-mail address just for online recruitment so your current inbox doesn't get overloaded. Most volunteer opportunity lists are free, so put opportunities on multiple sites.

2. **Make sure your website is recruitment friendly.** Put a visible link, like a highlighted box, to your volunteer page on every page of your website: home, other departments, etc. Beyond that have the link list available, volunteer opportunities and an online application. Make signing up to volunteer online as easy as possible.

3. **Create a newsgroup.** A newsgroup is like an online community where its members can chat, receive notices, etc. You can create your own site for your volunteers and direct prospective volunteers to it. Newsgroups

can also be searched based on topic. Check out groups. google.com for an online tour and instructions to set up your own group.

Volunteer Opportunities Websites

Some websites dedicated to volunteering include:

Network for Good — www.networkforgood.org

VolunteerMatch — www.volunteermatch.org

Craig's List — www.craigslist.org

1-800 Volunteer — www.1-800-volunteer.org

Monster.com — http://volunteer.monster.com

Idealist — www.idealist.org

Volunteer Solutions — www.volunteersolutions.org

U.S.A. Freedom Corps — www.usafreedomcorps.gov

National Mentoring Partnership — www.mentor.org

ServeNet — www.servenet.org

---

2. vMentors — A Program Making a Big Difference

These days many nonprofit organizations use virtual volunteers — persons who work from a computer either on site or from home to fulfill a volunteer role.

One such nonprofit is the Orphan Foundation of America (OFA) of Sterling, VA.

OFA staffs 300 virtual volunteers to mentor teens with its vMentor program. This cognitive coaching matches teens in the OFA program with mentors who are interested in their success and guidance for their futures.

Founded in 1981, OFA serves thousands of foster teens across the United States. With the help of vMentors, 366 of those teens are given guidance by adult vMentor volunteers by way of e-mail dialogue, guiding the teens to make good decisions.

"We don't want the mentors to answer their questions, we want the mentors to guide the mentees to create their own answers," says Lynn Davis, manager of partnership development for OFA.

How can your organization best utilize virtual volunteers?

- **Offer a structured training program** — Volunteers working within the vMentor program must complete

an extensive virtual training program and participate in monthly trainings to volunteer as mentors to OFA teens. Mentors are trained to guide students to draw their own conclusions instead of offering them a direct answer to the problem.

- **Monitor all communications** — In OFA's case, all communications are done on secure portals and are monitored by staff to ensure the safety of the mentored teens.

- **Offer ongoing training and consistent contact with virtual volunteers** — vMentor volunteers participate in monthly trainings and support sessions headed by OFA staff to keep the program on track.

Participation in the vMentor program is a decision made by the teen. Teens mentored within the vMentor program are twice as likely to graduate than those who do not accept mentoring, says Davis, noting: "vMentors help our kids stay motivated to stay in college."

Lynn Davis, Manager of Partnership Development, Orphan Foundation of America, Sterling, VA. Phone (571) 203-0270. E-mail: ldavis@orphan.org. Website: www.orphan.org

3. Essential Elements of a Volunteer Web page

How does your volunteer Web page measure up? Four essential elements to include:

1. **A noticeable link from your agency's home page to your volunteer page(s)** — if website visitors land on your homepage, provide an obvious link to volunteer opportunities. Check out the index of links on the home page of **Gulf Coast Jewish Family Services (Clearwater, FL)** for an example (www.gcjfs.org).

2. **Easily accessible contact info** — for an example, see the **Minnesota Historical Society's** Web page (www.mnhs.org/about/volunteers).

3. **Location** — offer a map or driving directions along with where to park and where to enter your offices once visitors arrive. **Presbyterian Hospital of Plano (Plano, TX)** offers location information and maps on its site (go to www.texashealth.org and click "Find Maps/Directions" under "What Do You Want to Do?").

4. **Ways volunteers can help** — list types of volunteer opportunities. Enable website visitors to click on each item to receive more details about what's involved. Check out **Harbor Medical Center's (Seattle, WA)** Web page (http://uwmedicine.washington.edu/Patient-Care/Locations/HMC/Community-Relations/volunteer/Pages/default.aspx).

4. Consider Your Website's Audience Before Making Changes

Before making major changes to your website, think through how doing so may impact your frequent online visitors, especially those who may not be computer savvy.

For example, if many of your supporters are 65 or older, have you researched to determine the best elements to make Web browsing simple for this target audience?

Aaron Howard, senior Web designer at IlluminAge (Seattle, WA), a communications firm specializing in needs of organizations that serve older adults and caregivers, says that when evaluating a website's effectiveness as a tool for reaching older adults, ask:

Are your site's organization and navigation clear?

Can users readily tell what's on the site by looking at the homepage? If they go to another page, can they figure out how to get back home? To ease navigation, use consistent layout and symbols, and locate top-level navigation buttons in the same place on each page.

Is type readable?

Use a sans serif font, no smaller than 10-point. Remember, dark type on a white background is easiest to see. Double-space and left-justify body text. If possible, allow users the option to adjust type size.

Are links and other navigation signals clear?

Text with links should be underlined and in a contrasting color. Visited links should then change to a third color. Never underline non-linked text.

Are interface elements suitable for older users?

Links and buttons should provide a forgivingly large target

Website Elements to Avoid

Make your website simple to navigate, especially for visitors 65 and older or with visual impairments.

According to Aaron Howard, senior Web designer, IlluminAge (Seattle, WA), "Many of the 'bells and whistles' that Web developers love can actually hinder the ability of older adults to navigate and comprehend your site."

To keep your website accessible to more people, he says, avoid:

- **Elaborate fly-out menus.** These require precise, coordinated mouse clicks that can be a nightmare for people with arthritis or tremors.

- **Fashionable patterned backgrounds.** These can make text unreadable for older eyes.

- **Large video downloads.** These files can often bring older model computers to a grinding halt.

---

for users whose level of manual dexterity doesn't allow them to zero in on precise spots.

Is text designed with senior readers in mind?

Shorter paragraphs, few complex sentences and plenty of subheadings and other visual cues help readers process the information. In writing for the Web, less really is more.

Source: Aaron Howard, Senior Web Designer, IlluminAge, Seattle, WA. Phone (800) 448-5213. E-mail: aaron@illuminage.com

5. YouTube Channel Puts University Research Front and Center

How would you like to share your work and get your message out to 500 people a day? That's what a branded YouTube channel (www.youtube.com) is accomplishing for Purdue University (Lafayette, IN), according to Mike Willis, staff member with Purdue's online experience and emerging technologies group, Office of Marketing and Media.

Purdue's public information and media relations staff started using the channel after noticing other research universities — including the University of California, Berkeley — were doing so successfully.

With the help of the public relations office at Berkeley and YouTube staff, Purdue staff created their own presence on the popular video-sharing site.

In most cases, university officials post videos that are produced in conjunction with news releases put out by the university, Willis says. "Other areas of the university provide some material," he says, "but the basic idea is to not put up video that we would be embarrassed to see on the local TV stations."

They include links to the videos in news releases sent to media and published on Purdue's website. A faculty/staff newsletter also lists links to news releases and videos.

Statistics provided through YouTube analytics (which also tell how viewers locate videos and basic demographic information) show Purdue videos are viewed 500 times per

---

Setting Up a Branded YouTube Channel

Thinking about how your organization can get started with YouTube (www.youtube.com)?

The site has a program for nonprofits to create their own branded channels.

The program, for eligible nonprofits in the United States and United Kingdom, provides premium branding capabilities and uploading capacity. It also gives the option to drive fundraising, place a call-to-action overlay on videos and post on the YouTube Video Volunteers' Platform to locate a skilled YouTube user to create your video.

For more information on how to maximize your YouTube channel to benefit your cause, visit www.youtube.com/nonprofits.

---

day. YouTube also uses Purdue's channel as a good example of a university channel.

Willis suggests making sure you have a plan for providing updates and new material for the channel if considering pursuing this form of information sharing.

Source: Mike Willis, Online Experience and Emerging Technologies Group, Office of Marketing and Media, Purdue University, West Lafayette, IN. Phone (765) 494-0371. E-mail: jmwillis@purdue.edu

---

6. Web-based Tools Help Manage Volunteers

Web-based tools are an effective way to manage volunteers from far away. In fact, for Stephanie Boyer, field services manager, Spina Bifida Association (Washington, DC), the goal was to make her online tools — an intranet site and listserv — the most important communication tools for the local chapters.

The intranet site, Leaders Online, hosts valuable information each chapter can use: job descriptions, templates for events and policies, nationwide funding; grants, marketing/promotion, and spina bifida fact sheets. The listserv provides a forum for the chapters to share resources and ask questions.

"We want to keep chapters engaged, informed and involved. These are major communication tools to do that," says Boyer.

Boyer moderates the listserv and uses it to remind

chapters to visit Leaders Online. Each member on the listserv receives a biweekly update. The updates provide the chapters with a brief overview of what new or updated information has been added to the site, which is important to create buy-in. The volunteers can quickly see if any of the information interests them and then visit Leaders Online for more information.

Still evolving, Boyer says chapter use of the Web tools has really grown over the last six months. Chapters share resources, so no one has to reinvent the wheel and it saves Boyer from repeating the same information everyone should know.

Source: Stephanie Boyer, Field Services Manager, Spina Bifida Association, Washington, DC. Phone (800) 621-3141 ext. 21. E-mail: sboyer@sbaa.org

7. Website Provides Help on Measuring Performance

Confused about measuring outcomes and how to use program logic models, inputs and outputs?

Log on to Corporation for National and Community Service's website and check out Project STAR, www. nationalserviceresources.org/star/st-comm/.

Project STAR provides tools, guides and examples for measuring performance for AmeriCorps, Senior Corps, State Commissions and Learn and Serve America groups. There are even puzzles to help you better understand how your inputs fit into a logic model.

8. Podcasts Reach More Volunteers, Supporters

Podcasts are growing in popularity as a means to promote nonprofit efforts, communicate volunteer opportunities and recruit volunteers.

One of the first volunteer centers to host a podcast, Volunteer San Diego (VSD) of San Diego, CA, has become a leader in utilizing social media. Volunteers at VSD have initiated and implemented these efforts, helping to expose thousands of new persons and entities to the nonprofit's services.

For its first podcast alone, VSD started out with about 100 downloads per month, says Brent Shintani, podcast producer for VSD. "We've since raised it to 30 to 70 downloads per day with more downloads right after each new posting. To date, we've had more than 20,000 downloads in total from our website."

Shintani answers questions about how podcasting benefits VSD's volunteer initiatives.

What is the purpose of the podcasts offered by VSD?

"Initially it was an experiment to reach a new, untapped audience. After that it became another platform for messaging to a different kind of audience — folks who listen to iPods and mp3 players. (It is also) a new way of delivering content to volunteers, volunteer managers and anyone interested in what we do. We received an early response from a volunteer center interested in service-learning in Maine — podcasts allow us to reach an audience beyond San Diego, even overseas!"

Who are podcasts meant for?

"Anyone interested in volunteering or needing volunteers. The great thing about podcasts is that you can tailor them to a specific audience, but you are online so anyone can become your audience."

Is there a cost to view them?

Tips to Make the Most of Podcasts

Having had significant success in using podcasts to promote volunteer initiatives at Volunteer San Diego (San Diego, CA), Brent Shintani, podcast producer, shares tips for creating and using attention-grabbing podcasts to the fullest:

- **Have a focused vision for the show.** Create a consistent theme for each podcast and always engage viewers with the mission of your organization.

- If looking at production value, it's always best to **have different points of view on a variety of different topics** — get the experts involved! Go to those who know the most and are the most passionate about what you're talking about in your podcast. Create a relaxed atmosphere and just talk. VSD has had great success using an interview format.

- **Try to keep to a consistent schedule to maintain your audience.**

- **Keep topics broad, but offer a timely message.** Podcasts allow you to cover similar topics while adding relevancy with specifics from organizational messaging for a certain time period (e.g., holiday volunteer opportunities or President Obama's call to service).

- **Deliver in any and all mediums.** Don't limit your organization to iTunes or specific feeds. Post everywhere — your organization's website, blog, Facebook, etc. By cross-posting, you can reach a wider audience.

"There is no cost to download."

How are the podcasts helpful to your organization and its constituents?

"Podcasts make volunteering accessible. They add a voice to volunteers and those involved to get others excited and engaged. For some, hearing about other's experiences inspires them to get involved. For volunteer managers and nonprofits, we discuss best practices and anecdotal program support. It provides an informal legitimacy to our information and a community for those interested in service."

Sources: Brent Shintani, Vice President of the Board and Podcast Producer; Kelli Ochoa, Development Director; Volunteer San Diego, San Diego, CA. Phone (858) 636-4133. E-mail: kochoa@volunteersandiego.org

9. Five Great Website Ideas

Here are five great website ideas to help improve your volunteer program:

1. **Online volunteer training.** Deb Jones, extension specialist, 4-H Volunteer Development (Logan, UT), worked with a Web designer to create a fast, easy online program on volunteer training basics. Prospective volunteers input contact information at www.utah4-H.org and are immediately linked to training modules. Training is in steps to help them gauge their interest. It is also a marketing tool; contact information goes to appropriate 4-H contacts.

2. **Discussion forum.** Jones says 4-H volunteers across Utah wanted a way to bounce ideas off each other and ask questions. So she and Utah State University information technology staff developed a simple, interactive blog-like online discussion forum where volunteers can pose questions and get immediate responses.

3. **Resource library.** Jones assembled years worth of useful volunteer information into a searchable online database where visitors can look for and download 4-H-related documents, handouts, resources and materials.

4. **Volunteer opportunities guide.** www.bloomington.in.gov/volunteer, lists volunteer opportunities available through the City of Bloomington (IN) Network, says Bet Savich, director. The site is constantly updated and each listing provides a description of the organization, opportunity and contact information.

5. **Interest and skills index.** This works in conjunction with the guide, above, to help volunteers choose positions that best fit them. The index lists all areas of interest (e.g., environment, education, animals) and then links each area with the matching opportunities available.

Sources: Deb Jones, Extension Specialist,
4-H Volunteer Development, Logan, UT. Phone (435) 797-2202.
E-mail: deb.jones@usu.edu. Website: www.utah4-H.org
Elizabeth (Bet) Savich, Director, City of Bloomington Volunteer
Network, Bloomington, IN. Phone (812) 349-3472.
E-mail: volunteer@bloomington.in.gov

10. Inform Your Top Officials of Volunteer Happenings

Do you keep your organization's top management informed of the valuable work volunteers are doing?

Officials with The Nebraska Medical Center (Omaha, NE) recently launched an e-newsletter, *Volunteer Notes,* to keep hospital management and service area coordinators abreast of volunteer news.

Every other month, 50 to 60 hospital personnel receive the two-to four-page e-newsletter, says Patricia Ostronic, lead, guest and volunteer services. The newsletter features upcoming volunteer events, articles on policies and procedures, new service area announcements, information on integrating volunteers into a department's team, recognition of volunteer efforts, department contact information and a services questionnaire.

Ostronic says ineffective communication methods were not getting the news out to hospital management. For years the volunteer office held bi-annual meetings with low attendance, sent memos only if there was something of real importance and held one-on-one meetings as needed.

"Our hospital does a great deal of e-mail communication, and I knew I would be able to get to hospital personnel more efficiently and quickly," she says. "The more informed the readers are in how our department and the in-service volunteers can assist them, the more comfortable they will be in utilizing the services provided as well as including the volunteers as a member of their team."

Ostronic says it's also important to share information with management that can be used to quantify the volunteers' service.

Source: Patricia Ostronic, Lead, Guest and Volunteer Services,
The Nebraska Medical Center, Omaha, NE. Phone (402) 559-4162.
E-mail: postronic@nebraskamed.com

Content not available in this edition

The Nebraska Medical Center's top management receives a monthly e-newsletter.

11. Offer Volunteer Publications to Serve Community, Nonprofits

Depending on the nature of your volunteer-driven organization, you may be able to provide a public service — and increase your visibility and ability to recruit volunteers — by offering publications that provide useful information.

The Volunteer Center Serving Howard County (Columbia, MD) offers community members, volunteers and nonprofits polished publications filled with useful and detailed information about area nonprofit organizations.

Volunteer center staff published the "Volunteer Opportunities to Mentor, Tutor & Educate 2009" and the "Volunteer Opportunities for Teens — May 2009" as resource guides for those looking for volunteer opportunities and to create an outlet where nonprofits could list their most updated information. In addition, the center produces an annual "Holiday Guide to Giving" that includes volunteer opportunities as well as holiday giving ideas. The teen guide is updated three times a year and the others are updated annually.

The publications are offered in PDF and Issuu formats (see box) on the center's website. Hard copies are printed in controlled quantities and reprinted when scheduled updated versions are created.

Mickey Gomez, executive director, offers tips to keep your publications fresh and up to date:

✓ Avoid duplicating efforts. Contact listed organizations for updates in advance of the publication dates and use that information for all resources listing that agency. For example, if an organization is supplying updates for the "Teen Guide", the volunteer center will also update that information in their 1-800-Volunteer search engine.

✓ Ask featured nonprofits to submit information in writing. E-mail your request with an attached form for the organization to complete and return as a printable document.

This prevents misinterpretations of information or incorrect listing data.

✓ When requesting source updates, send the latest version of the information available for that source and request updates. If a source requires no updates, ask them to return an e-mail stating that to keep on file.

✓ Offer visually appealing publications. Center staff change the covers of publications annually to distinguish publications from year to year and boost readership rates.

✓ Avoid producing hard copies in large quantities. Print as needed to keep current.

✓ Be sure to offer publications online in PDF form or by creating it in Issuu as online access is becoming the preferred method of viewing publications by constituents.

Source: Mickey Gomez, Executive Director, Volunteer Center Serving Howard County, Columbia, MD. Phone (410) 715-3172. E-mail: mickey@volunteerhoward.org

> ### About Issuu's Free Service...
>
> Issuu (www.issuu.com) lets nonprofits create online documents that allow users to electronically turn pages. The process can be done by uploading existing documents. The free service also lets you post Issuu documents online. To see sample documents, go to www.issuu.com, click "Publications," then "Nonprofits & Activism."

12. Canadian-based Website Offers Resource Assistance

Need some ideas to help develop a successful volunteer program? Want to see what works for other volunteer managers?

Canadian-based website www.volunteercalgary.ab.ca offers an online resource center free to volunteer managers. The website hosts topics in volunteering such as trends, training, success stories, policies and links to books, articles and seminars.

In particular, the website has a special section on developing policies and procedures, including a template. It provides definitions about policies and procedures, plus it includes a multitude of samples of strategies so you can put its experience to work for your own volunteer program.

In addition to finding this valuable information, you can read stories from other volunteer managers to see what has worked for them.

13. Go Green: Use Website to Save Time, Resources, Environment

The need to save both financial resources and maximize time constantly challenges any volunteer manager. Here's an effort that is helping one nonprofit do both:

In a move to go green and save on paper, mailing and other costs related to producing printed pieces, Lee County Parks and Recreation (Fort Myers, FL) now posts most volunteer-related information online, says Kathy Cahill, volunteer services coordinator. The switch came as they sought to revamp their website to recruit, recognize and reward volunteers and — as mandated by the county — cut their paper budget by 50 percent.

By placing documents online, Cahill says they cut their paper budget by 80 percent.

The website now contains:

✓ Updated information on number of volunteers and volunteer hours.

✓ A list of volunteer opportunities.

✓ A way to sign up for the e-mail mailing list.

✓ Pictures of volunteers in action.

✓ Downloadable volunteer applications, handbooks, brochures and the incentive program catalog.

✓ The quarterly newsletter, "The Volunteer Times."

Moving the newsletter from a paper to an electronic format saved major costs and time by itself, Cahill says. Previously, 1,000 volunteers received a 12-page newsletter in the mail.

While Cahill still mails newsletters to a handful of volunteers (per their request), she says many volunteers prefer to access them online. The online resource is especially helpful to volunteers who are snowbirds, in Florida just during the winter months.

Making the website a resource for volunteers also saves Cahill time. For example, when volunteers call, she can talk about their interests and direct them to the website for full position descriptions.

Source: Kathy Cahill, Volunteer Services Coordinator, Lee County Parks and Recreation, Terry Park, Fort Myers, FL. Phone (239) 432-2159. E-mail: kcahill@leegov.com

Tips for Creating, Updating Websites

Here are three ideas to create or improve your organization's website for little cost:

1. Use a free resource specializing in website design and hosting (e.g., www.myspace.com or www.freeweb.com) which allows you to upload content and is easy to set up and maintain.

2. Talk to your organization's information technology department or webmaster about suggestions to update your website. Explain what you want to do and ask for help to get it done.

3. Turn to people who grew up online: high school and college students. Kathy Cahill, volunteer services coordinator, Lee County Parks and Recreation (Fort Myers, FL), was interviewing a University of Florida student and simply asked her if she knew Dreamweaver software (for website design). The student had been using the software for years to help with a friend's business website. She came on as an intern and taught the staff how to use the software.

14. Company Makes E-communications Easy

If you're thinking about allocating more resources to e-communications, including e-mail updates and newsletters, use a company that knows the system well.

An increasing number of volunteer managers use Constant Contact (www.constantcontact.com) to send updates to their volunteers. The company offers customized nonprofit templates, including: newsletters, promotions, cards, invitations, holiday and seasonal e-mails and even online surveys.

Pricing depends on your e-mail list size. To send e-mails (newsletters, updates, etc.) to 1 to 500 volunteers, the cost is $15 a month, for 501 to 2,500, $30 a month. There are also special bundle discounts for using both the e-mail and survey features.

15. Social Media Strategies That Increase Visibility

Far from being a passing fad, social media is rapidly extending into the corporate and nonprofit sectors and changing the way stakeholders communicate with each other, and how they expect to communicate with your organization.

What is social media? It is using the Internet to instantly collaborate, share information and have a conversation about ideas, causes and organizations we care about powered by social media tools (e.g., social networking sites, blogs, podcasts, etc.).

Holly Ross, executive director, NTEN: The Nonprofit Technology Network (Portland, OR), says nonprofit communicators must understand how social media's newfound popularity will impact their cause and relay that to their constituency.

"As nonprofits, we're used to being authorities to our communities," Ross says. "Our role has been to decide what's important regarding our issues, to tell our community what matters, and to organize them to create change."

But the development of the Internet has forced nonprofits to change how they relate to their communities, she says: "First, the Internet has made accessing information incredibly easy. If you want to know about logging in your state, Google will tell you what's going on. Second, the Internet has made it ridiculously easy for us to share that information with each other, and to organize around that information.

"What that means is that people don't need us to tell them what matters. They don't need us to organize them. So as nonprofits our value proposition has shifted. We need to learn how they are using these tools to organize themselves, and what they are saying about our issues so we can understand what value we can bring to them."

Ross emphasizes that nonprofit communicators should think of social media as a series of steps that must be taken to increase visibility:

1. **Listen and participate in conversations that are already happening.** First, find out and listen to what people are talking about regarding the issues about which you care. How are they talking about the issues? What's motivating them? Next, use that knowledge to share your own insights and resources.

2. **Share your story.** Once you have a feel for the conversation, get your own story out there via blogs, podcasts, videos, etc. and invite the community to participate. Be brave and create content that is appropriate for your audiences and encourages feedback and conversation.

3. **Generate buzz.** Use sites like Facebook, StumbleUpon, Digg and Twitter to tell the world about what you're up to. Build a community of peers on these sites that will help you get the word out about your stories to their networks.

"The key to all these is community," says Ross. "You have to build real relationships with real people to make it work. That means that you'll have to contribute as much as you take, and you'll have to be open to whatever the community wants to tell you."

Source: Holly Ross, Executive Director, NTEN: The Nonprofit Technology Network, Portland, OR. Phone (415) 397-9000. E-mail: holly@nten.org

Social Media's Challenges

Like many forms of communication, social media has its pros and cons, says Holly Ross, executive director, NTEN: The Nonprofit Technology Network (Portland, OR).

Ross offers an example of how social media has changed communications for the better in terms of speed and scope: "We always wanted to create that perfect viral e-mail that would get forwarded around the Web. Adding 25 people to an e-mail send list is tedious compared to adding a link to Digg (www.digg.com). Getting your networks to tell a friend is all about capitalizing on their emotions in the moment. The easier that is, the more you'll get out of it. And social media makes it very easy."

While social media has helped in this manner, she notes it isn't a panacea. Its pitfalls include:

✓ **Presenting challenges to an organization's many cultures.** "To successfully implement a social media strategy, your organization must be prepared to behave in new ways. You have to be much more open and transparent than many organizations have been up to this point. The idea of accepting comments on a blog is abhorrent to many organizations, for example. They can't bear the idea of someone saying something negative."

✓ **Lack of control.** "The biggest mistake I see organizations make is the attempt to control their social media strategy too much. That's not how social media works. You can't delete negative comments. You have to respond to them honestly and openly."

✓ **Social media structure vs. organizational structure.** "We're used to working in departmental silos; programming does program work, fundraising raises money, marketing tells our stories. Social media combines elements of all of those. The folks implementing social media strategies are crossing departments more frequently, challenging our old ways of getting work done."

16. Website Targets Baby Boomer Volunteers

Many organizations have websites devoted to their volunteers, but what about to a targeted sub-group of volunteers?

A baby boomer website is what Elaine Hanson, director, RSVP (Forest City, IA) and Liz Weinstein, independent consultant, Elizabeth Weinstein and Associates (Urbandale, IA) developed as a way to communicate opportunities with volunteers participating in their baby boomer project. (Baby boomers are persons born between 1946 and 1964.)

When the four counties her organization serves were met with tight social service budgets and an increased need for quality volunteers, Hanson says, she collaborated with Weinstein to formulate the baby boomer project.

As part of the project to increase the number of volunteers in those counties by five percent in two years, they created the website, www.boomersinaction.net.

"A crucial part of the project is two-fold: to recruit baby boomer volunteers and to educate the general public about baby boomers and the significant role they can play in volunteerism," says Hanson. "The website will accomplish both goals."

The boomer-friendly site, launched in April 2008, features straightforward, factual information including pages dedicated to boomer stories, volunteering benefits and boomer news.

Visitors to the site can also find a list of volunteer opportunities available through RSVP and its partner nonprofits, as well as site links to the Iowa Commission on Volunteer Service, the Corporation for National and Community Service and the United Way of North Central Iowa.

Source: Elaine Hanson, Director, RSVP, Forest City, IA.
Phone (641) 585-8294. E-mail: hansone@waldorf.edu

17. Virtual Tour Provides Answer to Communication Challenge

Staff with North Texas Food Bank (Dallas, TX) had a challenge: to get people to realize they weren't a cozy little food pantry, but a major distribution center helping thousands of people.

The solution: a virtual tour on the food bank's website that would tell a story about the organization's day-to-day realities.

Colleen Townsley Brinkmann, chief marketing officer, says that after seeing a virtual tour on another website, she thought the tool could help them overcome the misconception most people had about the food bank.

Enter Ryan Iltis, owner, Green Grass Studios (Dallas, TX), who offered to create a virtual tour and underwrite any expenses.

Iltis and his team shot footage in one day, created the virtual video in two days and developed a virtual tour that shows the food bank's facilities, including the community kitchen and distribution center.

Iltis shares how the virtual tour came together:

- Food bank staff were put in charge of making sure the warehouse was staged and full of food to tell the most compelling story.
- Areas that would make the greatest impact were selected to be photographed.
- Iltis and his team arrived for the one-day shoot to capture the video.
- They color-corrected and stitched footage together to create the virtual tour.
- The virtual tour was uploaded to the organization's website.

Brinkmann says launching the virtual tour in mid-2007 has given the organization an inexpensive way to communicate its message to the average 50,000 users that visit the site monthly and, most importantly, "gives people a much more realistic view of what we do."

View the online tour at: http://www.ntfb.org/au_virtual_tour.cfm

> ### Choosing a Firm to Create Your Virtual Tour
>
> When hiring a firm to create a virtual tour, ask these questions, says Ryan Iltis, owner, Green Grass Studios (Dallas, TX):
>
> 1. Do you have Web experience?
> 2. Do you have experience stitching and creating 360-degree panoramic photography?
>
> He says average cost to create a virtual tour is $1,500 to $3,500.

Sources: Colleen Townsley Brinkmann, Chief Marketing Officer, North Texas Food Bank, Dallas, TX. Phone (214) 347-9594.
E-mail: colleen@ntfb.org
Ryan Iltis, Owner, Green Grass Studios, Dallas, TX.
Phone (214) 880-0101. E-mail: riltis@greengrassstudios.com

18. Buzz Groups Promote Exchange of Ideas

If you're training a large group of volunteers, make use of buzz group sessions to break the monotony and foster learning among your participants.

Here's how it works: divide participants into small groups that meet for a short time, usually as part of a longer training session. The group considers a simple question or problem, offering ideas and solutions. Ideas from each smaller group are then presented to the total group to promote further discussion.

> **Buzz groups are particularly helpful:**
> ✓ When the group is too large for everyone to participate.
> ✓ When studying more complex subjects.
> ✓ When time is limited.

Buzz groups are different than brainstorming because they generally emphasize problem solving.

19. Eight Tips for Writing Engaging Website Copy

Whether launching a new website or redesigning an existing one, keep some key tips in mind when developing the all-important copy that will fill your Web pages.

Joyce Remy, senior editor with the communications firm, IlluminAge (Seattle, WA), offers information that can help nonprofits create website content that both meets the needs of Web users while getting the most value from their website investment:

1. **Consider the other reader — the search engine.** For search engines to find website pages, the pages must include keywords likely to be used by people trying to find your organization. If your organization is a food bank, use terms on your site such as "feeding the hungry" and "food shelf." "As you craft copy, it is important that your keywords sound natural to the readers," says Remy. "If it looks like you've seeded your text with keywords, your site will seem less trustworthy."

2. **Web users are usually seeking a particular piece of information.** Unlike a brochure or ad, websites come with high expectations as an information source, Remy says. "Tailor your language accordingly, offering customers concrete facts, engagingly presented, about all the services your organization offers."

3. **Users navigate your site in a non-linear fashion.** Because Web users can move freely through the site, it is vital that your text doesn't depend on information found on previous pages. Make a good impression on every page, realizing that page users may arrive on a page other than your home page as they navigate the Web.

4. **Persons read Web pages differently than they read other types of copy.** Remy says studies indicate website visitors usually begin with a quick initial once-over when visiting a page. Visual cues such as short paragraphs, bullet points, subheads and white space ensure they can find what they want quickly.

5. **Compared to the printed page, reading on a computer screen is hard work.** As you begin constructing your text, write long and edit to short. Once you've captured your basic points, you can usually trim quite a bit and not lose the meaning. The recommended length for most Web pages is 200 to 400 words per page.

6. **The text of your website doesn't stand alone.** Elements such as logo and contact information, images, navigation buttons and consistent footers allow users to quickly figure out what is available on the site and constantly interact with your text. This can help keep copy concise.

7. **Hyperlinks add a new dimension.** This option allows readers to go to a different spot on the page, different page on your site or to another site entirely. "Hyperlinks give your users the choice of learning about something in greater depth, but don't overdo it," Remy says. "Links can be distracting and once readers leave a page, they may not return." Instead, embed links in a natural fashion, avoid using "Click here."

8. **Use website content area wisely.** Dedicate time to work on the copy, hire a copy-writer or ask colleagues and clients for feedback, suggests Remy. "Viewers may not know about your organization. Be clear, concise and thorough when describing the services, geographic areas served and your organization's history, staff or philosophy."

Source: Joyce Remy, Senior Editor, IlluminAge Communication Partners, Seattle, WA. Phone (800) 448-5213. E-mail: joyce@illuminage.com

20. Tips to Recruit Volunteers Online

Communicating in the online realm will catch the attention of a broader audience, including Generation Xers (born 1961-1981) and Generation Yers (born 1982-2001) who tend to readily use online technology. Here are three tips to recruit volunteers online:

1. **Send an e-blast to your contact list.** Send a notice to e-mail contacts that includes detailed information on your organization and the position you wish to fill. Include necessary contact information so persons can contact the appropriate person in your organization. Respond to e-mail inquiries in a timely fashion.

2. **Recognize current volunteers online.** By recognizing accomplishments of existing volunteers through e-blasts and on your website, you'll spotlight the positive approach your organization takes with volunteers and gain more interested potential volunteers.

3. **Announce openings on nonprofit message boards.** After careful research, post your need for volunteers and the description of the role you're looking to fill on appropriate message board sites to get the attention of those who frequent the site.

21. Online Site Helps Connect With College Volunteers

Looking for a go-to spot on college and university campuses to recruit volunteers?

Karen Partridge, communications manager, Campus Compact (Providence, RI), says they partner with more than 1,000 colleges and universities to help establish relations with community organizations across the country.

"Campus Compact helps build strong campus-community ties while providing volunteer managers a resource to recruit volunteers on campus," says Partridge.

Volunteer managers can utilize www.compact.org, to access the following resources:

- **Program models.** Visitors can access more than 700 established program models used by colleges and universities to create relationships with their community agencies.

- **Promise of Partnerships.** Partridge says the "Promise of Partnerships" is a volunteer manager's guide to

tapping into local colleges and universities' resources. The publication offers advice on making the right contacts, planning effective partnerships and working with students and faculty. The book also features tips, checklists and best practices.

- **Online volunteer opportunities list.** Community-based organizations can post their volunteer opportunities at: www.compact.org/opportunities/volunteer. Some 9,800 college students, faculty and campus community service directors visit the site weekly.

- **Search by state to locate colleges/universities.** The site offers volunteer managers the option to select the state in which they are interested and view their members.

Source: Karen Partridge, Communications Manager, Campus Compact, Brown University, Providence, RI. Phone (401) 867-3922. E-mail: kpartridge@compact.org

22. Start Your Own Online Discussion Group

If your organization has a website, consider creating a listserv as a way to promote communication and reflection among volunteers.

An online discussion group allows volunteers to share their thoughts and experiences. Participants can post questions to the group, suggest readings or ask for feedback on issues they are facing. Volunteer leaders and staff can request summaries of activities via e-mail and serve as moderators of the discussions. You can even compile a digest of e-mail

discussions and make it available to participants.

Anyone with an e-mail address who can be reached via the Internet can be added to the discussion group. Listservs are especially effective for large volunteer organizations or organizations with volunteers in multiple locations.

You can set up your own listserv through the Web on sites such as Yahoo Groups (http://groups.yahoo.com/) or Topica (http://lists.topica.com/).

23. Put Your Volunteer Program Online

Online Volunteering Opens Doors To Volunteers, Organizations

Is an online volunteer program right for your organization?

Lucking says their program has become a great volunteer resource for the Phoenix community with more than 350 agencies involved and more than 1,000 hits on the site weekly.

Lucking says many organizations and volunteers have turned to an online volunteer program for various reasons:

For the volunteer:
- ✓ If transportation is difficult.
- ✓ If they are limited physically.
- ✓ If people have commitments that require them to stay home yet they have the time and desire to volunteer.
- ✓ The freedom to schedule their time. Some individuals have schedules that allow them time to volunteer only when most agencies are closed.

For the organization:
- ✓ The online program reduces the cost of using paper and mail. A few clicks are more economical than spending resources for staff and supplies.
- ✓ It's easier to keep information updated.
- ✓ Online recruiting and volunteer registration provides accurate information about volunteers by storing it on electronic databases. This saves personnel time and improves program efficiency.
- ✓ The online program easily establishes electronic messaging as a powerful volunteer communications tool.

What's required to get an online volunteer program off the ground?

In 2000, Pit Lucking, coordinator, Arizona State University Volunteer Services (Phoenix, AZ), learned firsthand what it takes to get an online program up and running.

"The online part of the program started because I wasn't successful in getting the agency information out to the university community," she says. After realizing the university website would be her best chance to reach their target audience, the online volunteer program was launched.

If your organization is considering an online volunteer program, Lucking offers this advice:

1. **Evaluate your program needs.** After the program's goals and strategy have been evaluated, see how the Internet can assist in accomplishing various needs. "This practice assures the online volunteer program is aligned with the program's goals," she says.

2. **Recruit those needed to establish and maintain the program.** 1) Decide what will go onto the site and design the structure (internal links) within it; 2) Write each page of the site (e.g., information, forms, links, etc.); 3) Decide if any pages should be secure and how visitors will have access; 4) Work with a Web designer to make the site attractive and easy to manage; 5) Put the site online and manage it; and 6) Evaluate visitor traffic — from where visitors are coming, how long they view various pages, how many return to the site, etc.

3. **Locate agencies that want to be part of the program.** Lucking says at the university she and another volunteer contacted community agencies about the online program. Agencies were offered free advertising space and participation in a free campus volunteer fair. Now the site covers the entire valley and is used by metropolitan Phoenix as a volunteer information source, says Lucking.

4. **Get the word out.** With a limited budget, Lucking says her program relies on passing out website business cards, community and agency word of mouth, and Internet search engines to increase awareness among potential volunteers.

Content not available in this edition

Arizona State University Volunteer Services hands out business cards to promote its online volunteer program.

Source: Pit Lucking, Coordinator, Arizona State University Volunteer Services, Academic Community Engagement Services, Phoenix, AZ. E-mail: pit.lucking@asu.edu

24. Craft an Online Presence and Interactive Approach

The United Way of San Antonio and Bexar County (San Antonio, TX) offers a highly refined and effective interactive website, useful to both the volunteer and nonprofit organizations seeking to fill available positions.

The website (www.unitedwaysatx.org) offers a wealth of information for those seeking a volunteer opportunity. Here are three ways the website helps inform volunteers about the opportunities — ideas that could work for your organization's website:

- **Volunteer Solutions** — This section of the website currently lists 300 volunteer opportunities available in San Antonio and Bexar counties. Here, potential volunteers can search the database for the opportunity that best suits them. Volunteers can also save their areas of interest for faster future searches.

- **Special Events** — Volunteer drives and details are listed on the website to draw attention to the volunteer opportunities available through the United Way. For example, the Days of Caring event listing explains its goal of partnering with local businesses to offer a weekend's worth of project-based volunteer opportunities.

- **Ways of Caring Directory** — This online resource lists 200 agencies affiliated with the United Way of San Antonio and Bexar counties, offering a description of the agency, a list of typical jobs available at the agency, age requirements and other details useful to volunteers.

Esther Cantú, director of volunteer programs and services, says listing all of these items and more at the organization's website draws more attention to the volunteer opportunities and makes the volunteer process simple and well defined.

Realize the maximum potential of your website by listing specific opportunities, offering a volunteer search component, adding a resource database and emphasizing special volunteer events. This approach can save staff time and create an easy way for volunteers to access opportunities more readily. In turn, organizations in need of volunteers will fill those positions more quickly.

Source: Esther Cantú, Director of Volunteer Programs and Services, United Way of San Antonio and Bexar County, San Antonio, TX. Phone (210) 352-7000.
E-mail: ECantu@unitedwaysatx.org

25. Electronic Orientation Overcomes Scheduling Woes

One of the main challenges The Chester County Hospital's volunteer services office (West Chester, PA) faces when welcoming a new volunteer is scheduling orientation. Two obstacles hamper timely orientation attendance: scheduling a convenient time for day, evening and weekend volunteers, and the consumption of the staff and volunteers' time.

Using the power of a computer, the volunteer services staff found a solution to their problem — an electronic version of a volunteer orientation. Staff burned a CD of a PowerPoint presentation covering the hospital's mandatory topics (e.g., fire safety, HIPPA, infection control, patient safety and volunteer policies such as dress code and attendance). Short video clips were also embedded in the presentation to demonstrate hand-washing techniques and wheel chair safety. After each section, volunteers complete a short self-test on information they viewed in the orientation presentation. The completed test is filed in each volunteer's personnel file as confirmation of attendance. Volunteers receive a hard copy of the presentation, a customer service tip sheet, fire and disaster

procedures, and personal security tips as take-home support material.

The CD presentation allows increased flexibility for volunteers and staff. Volunteers view the presentation at their own pace, allowing for better comprehension of the material. Most volunteers complete the orientation in around 45 minutes. Volunteers may either view the orientation at volunteer services where a staff person is available to answer questions and assist volunteers who are not computer savvy, or the CD may be taken home.

"The electronic orientation presentation provides the opportunity to complete an obligation that would otherwise be daunting and time consuming in a more timely manner and at a convenient pace for hospital volunteers," says Kathy Stocker, director of volunteer services.

Source: Kathy Stocker, Director of Volunteer Services, The Chester County Hospital, West Chester, PA. Phone (610) 431-5191.
E-mail: kstocker@cchosp.com

26. E-mail Advice

When putting out an e-mail "call for help," send individual e-mails rather than a mass e-mail. If people see a request went to many others, they may feel less obligated to step forward and lend a hand.

27. Website Promotes Events

Upcoming.com is a site that allows nonprofits to promote events at no cost. The site sorts by city, allowing users to find events near their ZIP code. Get the word out about your next event, accessing a broader audience, with this online tool.

28. Website Showcases Volunteers of the Month

Almost every volunteer-driven organization has some sort of recognition program. So what sets yours apart from others?

For the Humane Society of Williamson County (Leander, TX), volunteers are thanked for their contributions on a truly worldwide scale — through the humane society's website.

What originated as a volunteer-of-the-quarter program became a monthly recognition when Memi Cardenas signed on as volunteer coordinator for the humane society.

"My decision to change the program was based on the fact that we have so many volunteers who do such great jobs that I would much rather recognize 12 than three," says Cardenas. "I think the more I can recognize and give back to them, the more we will create a stronger team."

Each month, Cardenas looks back over the previous month, gathering feedback from staff on who has excelled, made a difference or who has been volunteering for a long time but hasn't been acknowledged.

"The volunteer of the month can be someone who takes on a lot of responsibility as a team leader or someone who does something as simple, but appreciated, as walking the dogs a few times a week," says Cardenas.

The online profiles feature a photo and a biography highlighting the volunteer, what he/she has done for the organization and how long he/she has been volunteering.

Cardenas says the program is a great morale booster for her volunteers. "I have volunteers come up and ask me how they can become the volunteer of the month. It is a great

motivator to get the other volunteers to try and achieve that acknowledgement."

Source: Memi Cardenas, Volunteer Coordinator, Humane Society of Williamson County, Leander, TX. Phone (512) 260-3602, ext. 106. E-mail: mcardenas@hswc.net

Volunteer of the Month features on the Humane Society of Williamson County website include photos, biographies and reasons why volunteers are being honored.

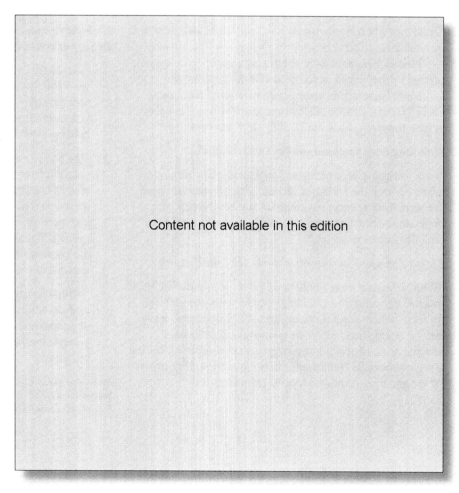

Content not available in this edition

29. Seven Tips for Launching Your Nonprofit's Facebook Page

To create a Facebook page and make sure it's a hit with your fans:

1. **Create a free user profile.** Go to facebook.com and click sign up. You'll fill out basic information, receive a confirmation e-mail and click the link in the e-mail. You now have a user profile.

2. **To create a Facebook page, go to www.facebook.com/ pages/create.php.** Type the name of the page exactly as you want it to appear and as you think users will search for it. Remember, you won't be able to change the name later.

3. **Select the category of your organization,** for example, a school would select education.

4. **Add content and publish your page.** Choose information that showcases your staff, donors and volunteers.

Remember, the stronger the page you create, the more of an effect it has on viewers.

5. **Update your page frequently.** The more often you add new content, the more often people will come back to your page. You can also send updates to your fans to announce news and events.

6. **Harness the power of news feeds.** News feeds on user home pages tell them what their friends are doing. When a user becomes your fan, the news feed feature tells their friends and invites them to become fans, too, which can lead to alumni and friends connecting to your nonprofit.

7. **Choose the application best for you.** While your page comes installed with basic applications, you can build your own applications that are more useful to your constituents.

30. Online Tool Helps Recruit, Track, Coordinate Volunteers

Could the right software program or online tool save time and increase your effectiveness?

One such online tool is Volgistics (www.volgistics.com), offered by the Volgistics company (Grand Rapids, MI).

Carla Hummel, director of volunteer services, Avera Sacred Heart (Yankton, SD), shares how she uses the online system to recruit, track and coordinate volunteers:

How long have you been working with Volgistics?

"I am just going on a year with Volgistics. It has been quite a step up from the Microsoft Access program we once used. We were finding ourselves continuously bombarded with more lab requirements and were really maxed out of space with the Access program."

Please describe how Volgistics works for your nonprofit.

"With Volgistics we not only have the room to grow but have much better control over adding requirements, developing levels of patient contact, managing several locations, easily pulling reports that help in decision-making processes, keeping track of pending requirements not completed, having always-accessible contact information and the ability to sort by assignments, locations, type of volunteer, etc."

Share three examples of how Volgistics has helped you as director of volunteer services:

1. "Just today I came from a brainstorming session where we were discussing starting a new volunteer program in a specific area. I was able to go into Volgistics and pull all volunteers from a geographic area so that we can send a mailing to generate interest.

2. "We had just started on Volgistics and our infection control committee needed information on how many volunteers would be impacted by requiring a vaccination. We were given specific parameters and were able to plug them into a report and come up with the number of volunteers who would need the vaccinations, consequently calculating the costs associated with the effort."

3. "With Volgistics, we have the standard reports for birthdays, labels and lists by assignment for scheduling or attendance. We also have the ability to flag service groups, auxiliary members, employees or specific programs."

Source: Carla Hummel, Director of Volunteer Services, Avera Sacred Heart, Yankton, SD. Phone (605) 668-8104. E-mail: chummel@shhservices.com

31. Five Ways to Attract Volunteers Via Your Website

Many volunteer-reliant organizations find that online recruitment is a great way of finding new people.

Wendy Bojin-Liston, manager of volunteer services, Special Olympics of Northern California (Pleasant Hill, CA), uses these steps to turn online inquiries into volunteers:

1. **Ensure site is easy to find**. Have your IT department review your website's metadata section for key words that will ensure your site will pop up during various Web searches. In addition, partner with volunteer organizations that exist to place volunteers where they are needed by creating links between your website and theirs.

2. **Make registration easy**. Keep the application short. Bojin-Liston advises, "Find out a little bit about the volunteer's interest so you can have the appropriate staff member follow up with them to get additional information."

3. **Respond to inquiries quickly**. The worst move an organization can make is to put time and money into online registration but neglect to establish its system for timely follow up. Waiting too long to contact potential volunteers could mean losing the volunteer to another organization.

4. **Give multiple options**. If possible, let volunteers choose between specific events or volunteering on an ongoing basis. Some volunteers may be dynamite but not able to make a long-term commitment. Also, supply job descriptions online so potential volunteers know the expectations of each opportunity and can better select those that fit.

5. **Be willing to make changes to your website**. When Special Olympics of Northern California couldn't find information on volunteers who had applied online, Bojin-Liston says they took action. "We fine-tuned our process to make it easier for volunteers and worked with our IT department to ensure applications were flagged for immediate attention." Bojin-Liston says volunteer feedback regarding the application process and a good relationship with the IT department are keys to success in online recruitment.

Key Metadata Search Words

To ensure your website appears in Web search results, include these keywords in the metadata section of your website:

- Volunteer opportunities
- Volunteering
- Helping people
- Event
- Entertainment
- Youth, Families, Kids and/or Environment

Source: Wendy Bojin-Liston, Manager of Volunteer Services, Special Olympics of Northern California, Pleasant Hill, CA. Phone (925) 944-8801. E-mail: wbliston@sonc.org

32. Inclusion is Key to Recognizing Virtual Volunteers

Not all volunteers work on site. Some work in remote offices, while others work in a virtual environment online. So how can you best recognize the service of volunteers with whom you have little or no physical contact?

In a virtual environment, recognition needs to be more of a conscious and planned act because there are not as many spontaneous opportunities to acknowledge a volunteer's hard work and accomplishments. Making sure a virtual volunteer stays motivated, happy and productive is the key to ensuring his or her success.

Often the best form of thanks is seeing and hearing what a difference the volunteer's work really makes. Here are some things you can do to show volunteers how their work contributes to your organization's mission:

- Add them to your online mailing list.
- Copy them on staff memos (as appropriate) relating to programs and services in which they might be interested.
- Invite them to special events, staff training and celebrations (if logistically possible).
- Invite their comments about programs and services; ask them about the volunteer program and how it's working for them.
- Make sure they have an open invitation to visit your agency when they're in town.

33. Use Electronic Bulletin Board to Recruit, Nurture Volunteers

Consider an electronic bulletin board as a means to recruit new volunteers. Electronic bulletin boards, commonly known as message boards or computer forums, are online communication systems to share, request or discuss information on any topic.

Through sites like VolunteerMatch.org, nonprofits post volunteer opportunities. When a person expresses interest in an opportunity, the organization receives an e-mail notification. The nonprofit must follow up and offer the person more information.

To maximize benefits of posting opportunities online, VolunteerMatch's website recommends including a specific, catchy title; a detailed description of the opportunity and what is expected of the volunteer; accurate date and time information and up-to-date contact e-mail address.

Three volunteer managers who use electronic billboards weigh in on their experiences:

"The Internet service I find that yields the most referrals for our organization is VolunteerMatch. The advantage is that you get a large number of volunteers who are interested in serving. In the last year, I would say VolunteerMatch has yielded at least 60 volunteer referrals directly and 90 indirectly (when a person who saw our posting contacted the office rather than making the referral online or were referred by a friend/family member). The disadvantage is that you have to court them more than you would people who are familiar with hospice. The other disadvantage is that you get a homogeneous group of technology savvy volunteers. As we know, organizations need volunteers of all types to be successful. I don't find that it's the best way to engage the leading-edge baby boomers or traditional volunteers."

— *Michelle Jones, Volunteer Coordinator, Bon Secours Hospice (Portsmouth, VA)*

"I have used volunteer recruitment websites such as VolunteerMatch and Volunteer Delaware to recruit volunteers. This has proven to be very helpful in getting volunteer interests, though the volunteers who sign up through these programs have not historically followed through and/or do not stay with the program long. They are typically people who use volunteerism to gain work experience and are gone as soon as they find a job. This is not necessarily a bad thing as long as you know that this is likely to happen so you can adjust your training and assignments. I typically ask these volun-

Online Electronic Recruitment Tools

Considering an electronic bulletin board to aid recruitment efforts? Here are a few options:

- **Network for Good** (www.networkforgood.org/Npo/volunteers/default.aspx)

- **Idealist** (www.idealist.org)

- **VolunteerMatch** (www.volunteermatch.org/post)

- **National Mentoring Partnership** (www.mentoring.org)

- **UNV's Online Volunteering Service** (www.onlinevolunteering.org)

- **SERVEnet** (http://servenet.org/)

- **1-800-volunteer.org** (www.1-800-volunteer.org/1800Vol/OpenIndexAction.do)

teers up front about their intentions and then assign them short-term projects they can do in one or two days at a time rather than setting them up and training them for ongoing jobs."

— *Edith Banning, Program Director, Kent/Sussex Adopt-a-Family (Milford, DE)*

"I'd say electronic bulletin boards are marginally effective because I've been using two to three bulletin boards for approximately three years and have had about 10 inquiries. Out of that group I have recruited and trained one volunteer who is no longer with the agency. However, I've had hundreds of visitors to our Web page bulletin board, a free posting that has increased name recognition for my agency, which in itself is worth the investment of time and energy to post on an electronic bulletin board. Even though I find electronic bulletin boards to be marginally effective, I'll continue to use this resource because I think there is a potential treasure trove of e-volunteer opportunities and volunteer services that can be provided via Internet communications and distant volunteers."

— *Vince Chiles, Hospice Supervisor, Covenant Home Care (Reading, PA)*

34. Make Online Connections Through Your Employers

Does your employer have a website? If so, explore ways to use that to your volunteer agency's benefit. Some possibilities include:

✓ Setting up a link from your employer's website to the volunteer agency.

✓ Including a public service message about the agency on your employer's website.

✓ Selling agency items through your employer's website.

✓ Announcing upcoming agency events through your employer's website.

✓ Making mention of the agency — and volunteer opportunities — in your employer's blog or e-newsletter.

35. Showcase Your Virtual Volunteering Options

Has your organization considered the world of virtual volunteering but you don't know where to begin?

Volunteermatch.org (www.volunteermatch.org) offers a virtual section that features volunteer opportunities for those who may be homebound, a single parent or who would rather donate time from the comfort of their home:

- Advocacy and human rights
- Animals
- Arts & Culture
- Board development
- Children & Youth
- Computers & Technology
- Disaster relief
- Education and literacy
- Homeless and housing
- Justice and legal
- Media and broadcasting

36. Online Conferencing System Helps Bridge the Gap

Is your organization struggling to connect volunteers separated by miles and busy schedules?

As the reunion gift coordinator for The College of St. Catherine (St. Paul, MN), Anne Lindberg was in search of a program that could simplify how she engages volunteers locally and nationally.

"Our alumnae are spread out across the United States. Therefore, we needed a way to meet simultaneously with local volunteers and those based elsewhere in the country," says Lindberg.

What she found was WebEx, an online Web conferencing system. "One person can be in San Francisco on a business trip, while another is at home. All they need is the Internet and a phone. WebEx allows people who have conflicting schedules to meet, discuss and strategize ideas in real time," says Lindberg.

"In the past, it could take weeks to plan a meeting around the schedules of our volunteers. Now a meeting can be scheduled and held within a few days. That quick turnaround was all but impossible before."

Conducting a meeting

To hold a meeting, Lindberg selects a meeting time and e-mails the volunteers an invite. WebEx then sends those individuals an e-mail with a link to the meeting website and a phone number to enter the meeting.

As the host, Lindberg can pull up any document on her computer. Participants view documents that Lindberg has on her screen through the WebEx interface. The program's capabilities include video conferencing and live chat. Participants attending the meeting can also edit documents in real time.

While WebEx can accommodate up to 50 people per meeting, Lindberg's meetings connect five to 10 volunteers on average.

Lindberg says WebEx's $130 monthly rate for the College of St. Catherine is based on a nonprofit rate for 500 minutes of meeting time.

Source: Anne Lindberg, Reunion Gift Coordinator, The College of St. Catherine, St. Paul, MN. Phone (651) 690-8854. E-mail: aklindberg@stkate.edu

37. Going Paperless Makes Teen Orientation Run More Smoothly

Think about how much paper your volunteer office uses for each volunteer: application forms, volunteer handbooks, guidelines, orientation materials, etc. Now think about how much of that information could be put online.

That's exactly what Jamine Hamner, coordinator of volunteer services, Saint Joseph Health Care (Lexington, KY) did. A year ago Hamner and her staff wanted to streamline the teen volunteer program from a two-day orientation to a two-hour orientation.

What they did was create a paperless office with an online application system that works for the entire volunteer program.

A volunteer can search the available opportunities, complete and submit the application directly online. The applicant then receives an e-mail with instructions to complete the orientation online. The orientation materials — a confidentiality agreement, multiple choice safety test, multiple choice HIPAA test, volunteer agreement and orientation checklist — are all completed online and signed by the volunteer through electronic signature. As the applicant submits each item, it goes to Hamner's e-mail. She calls the volunteer and sets up an interview. During the interview she gets the required background information and finishes up the orientation process. Once the volunteers begin placement, each has his/her own login and password to check schedules and updates.

One of the biggest advantages to going paperless is the lack of wait time a volunteer has between applying and starting. Before going paperless, Hamner says, the application process took about one month, depending on if the volunteer signed up right after the monthly orientation. Now the process takes a week.

Hamner admits the office isn't entirely paperless. They do mail paper copies of forms to volunteers when needed — about one every three months. Hamner still requires one ink-to-paper

Advice for Setting Up a Paperless Office

Jamine Hamner, coordinator of volunteer services, Saint Joseph Health Care (Lexington, KY) says her office went paperless through trial and error. Now, that she's done it, Hamner says she'd never go back.

Hamner offers a list of essentials an organization must have when converting to a paperless office:

- Internet connection from your work computer.
- A website that allow you to upload documents.
- Your documents in an electronic format (e.g., Word or PDF) that will be accessible.
- An online volunteer application that can be submitted from the website.
- Orientation forms, agreements, tests which can be created through your website.
- A separate place to store your electronic volunteer files, such as your organization's server or online file storage.
- A scanner with an automatic document feeder.

Hamner says before pursuing a paperless office it's important to ask your IT department if your website can support the transition. If not, Hamner says, by using a search engine organizations should be able to locate free and inexpensive options to create their own paperless office.

signature for the parental consent form for the teen volunteer program, which is accessible from the website.

Source: Jamine Hamner, Coordinator of Volunteer Services, Saint Joseph Health Care, Lexington, KY. Phone (859) 313-1290. E-mail: hamnerja@sjhlex.org

38. VRM Roundtable Extends Networking Options

The VRM Roundtable has a new registry that can help you stay connected to other nonprofit professionals. The Registry is an online professional listing of organizations that serve volunteer resource managers, including: formal and informal government, non-governmental organizations, faith based, volunteer centers, directors of volunteers in agencies, networks and state associations.

"The Registry is a central point where individuals can locate contact information for professional organizations in their area," says Celeste Sauls-Marks, leadership team leader. "The advantage of sharing this information is that organizations will be able to reach out and share information about their programming, membership levels and contact information."

It's free to post your contact information and you can update anytime from the VRM Roundtable website, http://vrm-roundtable.org.

Source: Celeste Sauls-Marks, Leadership Team Leader, VRM Roundtable, Dallas, TX.

39. Use All Options Available to Communicate With Volunteers

Volunteers lead full lives and have many demands on their time. Communicating with them effectively will ensure that your volunteer events are well managed and that volunteers receive all necessary information to stay on top of their assignments.

Use the following communications tools to reach your volunteers:

1. **Facebook** — Ask current and incoming volunteers to become fans of your organization's Facebook page so they can receive Facebook posts about upcoming volunteer opportunities at your nonprofit.

2. **Website** — Create an event-specific volunteer page at your organization's website where volunteers can get details about your cause, sign up for specific volunteer tasks and garner information about the event.

3. **E-mail blasts** — Use e-mail as your primary communication tool during event planning. Make messages detailed and specific. E-mail announcements to all volunteers involved in the event, to assign specific roles to each volunteer and to keep them posted about changes. Don't forget to add the critical information regarding when the volunteers should arrive, what attire they should be wearing and any items they will need to bring.

40. Volunteer Log-in Helps Office Run Smoothly

Keep your volunteer office running smoothly with the help of an online volunteer log-in.

By simply logging into a personalized account, volunteers at Cheyenne Mountain Zoo (Colorado Springs, CO) have access to a variety of information and forms, including applications, messages, schedules, hour log-ins and new volunteer opportunities.

Jacki Moore, education administrative assistant, says the online log-in service, provided by Volgistics (Bloomington, IN), helps make the office run more smoothly.

For instance, Moore says, volunteers no longer need to contact her to reschedule hours, and she can communicate new opportunities and other announcements.

The service also allows her to tally volunteer hours easily, says Moore, who noted the system's only downfall is the fact that not all volunteers have Internet access.

Source: Jacki Moore, Education Administrative Assistant, Cheyenne Mountain Zoo, Colorado Springs, CO. Phone (719) 633-9925. E-mail: jmoore@cmzoo.org

41. Boost Volunteer Contact by Tweeting With Twitter

For many nonprofit organizations, social networking is the new norm when communicating with volunteers and staff.

Twitter (www.twitter.com) offers a new way to communicate with a number of individuals simultaneously using instant messaging via text messaging or online. In lieu of sending multiple messages to a variety of individuals, Twitter lets you reach a number of people with a single message.

Individual Twitter messages are referred to as tweets.

While Twitter allows you to send messages to many individuals at one time, it also allows you to gain feedback from this same group.

Use Twitter within your nonprofit to:

- Allow volunteers to view a portion of your day.
- Take immediate polls from staff or volunteers to aid in decision making or implementing new ideas.
- Organize instant meetings called Tweet ups.
- Send positive messages about your nonprofit to a select group of volunteers.
- Send instant information to volunteers about changes in scheduling or new happenings at your nonprofit.
- Request that existing volunteers recruit a friend to volunteer.

42. New Web Program Helps Sort Information

Do you have so many websites bookmarked that it would take all day to go through them? Do you perform all your Web searches through Google and sort through all the resulting websites just to get one piece of relevant information? If so, consider downloading an RSS reader to help sort out new and relevant website information.

RSS, Rich Site Summary or Really Simple Syndication, is a special computer language that helps share and manage website content. Instead of visiting bookmarked Web pages for new information, that new information (e.g., updates, blogs, news headlines, etc.) is listed, with brief summaries or links, from one website or e-mailed to you — it's like a Web inbox.

You can also use RSS to share your website's content with everyone on the Web. By setting up your website with an RSS feed, it can be subscribed to and shared. Your organization's blogs and new content can be easily accessed and are spam-free through an RSS reader.

RSS requires a downloadable reader or aggregator and many are available for free. Once you have a reader, you can do a keyword search for specific RSS feeds and subscribe to relevant ones.

More and more websites are adding RSS buttons so you can immediately add them to your reader's list. For more information on RSS and downloadable readers, visit www.techsoup.org/rss.

43. Offer Virtual Volunteering Opportunities to Appeal to More Volunteers

More nonprofits are seeing the value of virtual volunteers — people who provide services via virtual means, such as the Internet.

At St. Louis Regional OASIS (St. Louis, MO), two volunteering positions that are primarily virtual — proofreader and journalist — help produce and market an 80-plus page catalog three times a year.

Candice Arriola, volunteer manager, describes the positions:

- **Volunteer Proofreader** — receives draft of catalog and specific proofreading focus (e.g., one reader may pay special attention to grammar, while another may seek out formatting inconsistencies or inaccurate information). Arriola says splitting tasks works well because each volunteer's task is based on his/her individual strengths. Volunteers return edited drafts within set time frame. Articles may receive additional revisions.

- **Volunteer Journalist** — assigned specific duties such as writing a feature about a volunteer. Volunteer reporter sets up the interview, writes the article and submits it to Arriola. All completed articles are run by the director of communications at the national level for final approval. Ongoing support and supervision is provided through calls, e-mail or in-person meetings.

Both positions require writing and/or proofreading expertise and Arriola says many volunteers step forward if they have these abilities. She also posted the opportunities online and in the catalog, and announced them at a continuing education writing course offered by the organization.

Source: Candice Arriola, Volunteer Manager, St. Louis Regional OASIS, St. Louis, MO. Phone (341) 963-2094. E-mail: carriola@oasisnet.org

This job description helps volunteers at St. Louis Regional OASIS understand duties associated with the virtual volunteering opportunities:

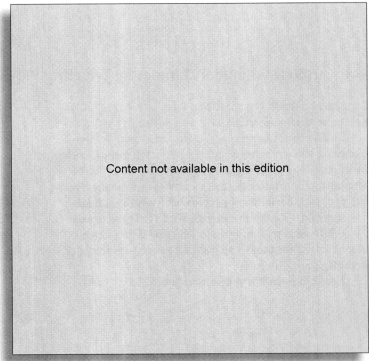

Content not available in this edition

44. Fresh Ideas to Drive Volunteers Into Nonprofit Organization

Sometimes all it takes is a fresh approach to find new volunteers.

When volunteer management staff with the Five Acres organization (Altadena, CA) were looking to fill open volunteer positions in two of its cottages that house children removed from their home by the courts, they came up with the idea of hosting a volunteer drive.

Pearl Kim, volunteer coordinator, organized the event following these steps:

❑ Sending mass e-mail invitations to the organization's contact list and publishing information about the event in local newspapers to invite guests to the drive.

❑ Asking staff to speak at the event to share their stories about the organization and the people they serve.

❑ Creating a digital storytelling video that shows testimonials by some of the children who were positively influenced by Five Acres. Sharing the testimonials makes the positive impacts of volunteering more of a reality, Kim notes.

❑ The night of the event, having staff mingle one-on-one with guests to reach out, share their stories and answer questions.

❑ Knowing that follow-up with guests would be crucial to securing them as volunteers, Kim suggests calling guests of your volunteer drive a few days after the event and inviting them to the next business meeting of your organization to keep your organization at the forefront of each potential volunteer's mind.

Of the guests who attended the Volunteer Drive event, 43 percent enrolled to become new volunteers for Five Acres.

"Volunteers are one of the most important aspects of growth and healing for the children here at Five Acres," Kim says. "A dedicated, consistent and compassionate adult can really change a child's life. My goal is to convey this message to people when presenting volunteer opportunities."

Source: Pearl Kim, Volunteer Coordinator, Five Acres, Altadena, CA. Phone (626) 798-6793. E-mail: pkim@5acres.org

45. Podcasts Tug at Heartstrings of Potential Volunteers

When visitors browse the Memorial Health System of Colorado Springs volunteer website, they're greeted by Janie, a longtime hospital volunteer, in the form of a new tool appealing to the emotions of potential volunteers — podcasts.

Chris Swanson, Web communications and marketing strategist, says podcasts go beyond the words that anyone can glance over and instead use a real person to get people to listen, and hopefully, volunteer.

Setting up a podcast is simple and cheap, Swanson says. Apple computer users may already have GarageBand software, while PC users can download the free software Audacity (http://audacity.sourceforge.net/) for everything needed to record and edit a podcast.

Be careful not to overproduce your podcast, Swanson advises. While hospital staff clean up interviews to take out dead air and sneezes, they leave in background noise and other ambience. By doing so, Swanson says, people are more likely to believe the podcast is just another person talking to them rather than a commercial.

Also, Swanson says, persons being interviewed should tell a story. Have them paint a picture — explain why they

volunteer and why others should do the same. This results in people putting more of a human element into their discussion, and people connect better with this.

A podcast can be completed in as little as an hour, but expect closer to two or three hours to interview, edit and upload the podcast to your website.

While Memorial Health System staff do not have statistics on how successful the podcasts are, Swanson says word-of-mouth indicates success. Doctors and others are lining up to be interviewed for podcasts to be put on other sections of the hospital website, Swanson says, adding that people want to be able to share it with their friends, family and colleagues.

Also, Swanson says, results of survey groups show people are reacting well to the Janie podcast as well as other podcasts on the hospital website.

Source: Chris Swanson, Web Communications and Marketing Strategist, Memorial Health System, Colorado Springs, CO. Phone (719) 365-2416.
E-mail: chris.swanson@memorialhealthsystem.com.
Website: memorialhealthsystem.com

46. E-news and Hot Sheets Take Place of Lengthy Newsletter

At the Denver International Airport (DIA) of Denver, CO, communication with volunteers is critically important.

But Corinne Christensen, administrator of DIA's hospitality ambassador program, found newsletters a cumbersome way to communicate with volunteers. So she created an electronic communications tool — Friday E-News bulletins, one-page handouts and hot sheets — to give volunteers up-to-the-minute updates to help them succeed.

Christensen answers questions about these new forms of volunteer communication:

What information is included in Friday E-News and what's included in hot sheets? How do they differ?

"Friday E-News is longer and contains the extra kind of news and computer items available to more than 260 volunteers, some employees and administration.

"E-News contains airport news and information (press releases, airline changes, passenger boarding forecasts, airport services updates, airport concessions and business updates, airport business updates that affect volunteers, events that involve the airport); community and tourist information (conferences traveling through the airport and their transportation information, events that include the airport); and volunteer program news and information (volunteer shift updates for the week, information about other airport volunteer programs, holiday information that affects the program, computer tips and fun searches, birthdays, programs news, volunteer anecdotes and thank-you notes, important dates).

"The hot sheet (shown below, right) is one-page, double-sided and more condensed with less detail, available for each shift during the week at shift meetings. The hot sheet contains press releases or timely airport news; motivating information for volunteers; shift information; airport updates and weekly dates."

How much time do you save doing this versus creating a typical newsletter?

"I save around a week's worth of time by doing the E-News on Fridays. I can include shorter amounts of information rather than the typical newsletter articles, which had to be edited by public information officers of our public relations division; they trust me to be informative, spell-checked and succinct!"

Who receives these communications? Are they geared to volunteers?

"The E-News and the hot sheet are geared for the volunteers, but our customer service employees and security officers like to have them simply because the airport no longer has a weekly newspaper. I double-check everything to make sure it is public

knowledge before I include that information in updates."

What are some specific tips you could share with other volunteer managers about creating these two publications?

✓ "Use the same format with each publication so your audience can check updated information at a glance.

✓ "Check your sources regularly to see where they are getting their information — I was once using a database that was waiting for my E-News to update the database — the information was going around in circles!

✓ "Add something personal in your news: a thank-you to a volunteer, a special anniversary date or something fun.

✓ "Include reminders that will help your great volunteers become wonderful volunteers.

✓ "Always include information that reminds volunteers of routine practices, such as, always take lost items to lost and found immediately or the website address of the volunteer program and the airport. I sometimes use these routine pieces as dividers between subjects and make them colorful and eye-catching."

Source: Corinne Christensen, Program Administrator, DIA Hospitality Ambassador Program, Denver, CO. Phone (303) 342-2243. E-mail: Corinne.Christensen@flydenver.com

Content not available in this edition

47. Get Tech-savvy Individuals to Set Up, Maintain Website

More and more nonprofits are looking to tech-savvy individuals to set up and manage their websites. But before asking anyone to take on that role — or to share that responsibility with others — create a position description such as the example shown at right.

By listing responsibilities, you can more clearly identify what's expected of anyone willing to fill or assist with the position. Additionally, anyone who considers helping will know what's expected.

In addition to IT professionals, don't overlook tech-savvy students (both high school and college-age) who can easily find their way around all sorts of technical devices and software.

You may find one person willing to take on the entire job or a handful of individuals willing to share the responsibilities. If it's the latter, be sure to spell out who's responsible for doing what and set occasional meetings for everyone involved to discuss issues.

Webmaster Job Description

Objective: To maintain the [name of organization] website. May include formatting and preparing weekly e-newsletter.

Time Commitment: Approximately 2-8 hours/week. Though much work can be done at any time of day from any location, webmaster will need to be accessible by phone and/or e-mail during regular business hours for urgent needs and occasional meetings.

Responsibilities:
- Receive and place content (text, photos, some PDFs to upload) regularly from [name of organization] staff.
- Update and maintain website on a weekly basis. Includes updating homepage, calendar events, posting news and monthly newsletters.
- Find new ways to utilize the website to communicate with constituents.
- Communicate and collaborate with staff on best use of the website for marketing and communications.

48. Volunteer Blog Promotes Communication

Create a volunteer blog exclusively available to your volunteer management team and your steadfast volunteers to streamline communication within your nonprofit. Consider these benefits of hosting a volunteer blog at your organization's website:

- Volunteer managers can communicate with all volunteers at one time regarding upcoming events, changes to policy, volunteer openings and more.
- Volunteers have unlimited access to updates within your nonprofit that directly involve them.
- Volunteer coordinators can post volunteer schedules for easy access.
- Volunteers can post status updates regarding their role in an upcoming event.
- Photos of volunteer activities can be easily uploaded to the site.
- Volunteers can recruit additional volunteers by talking up the blog to friends, family and colleagues.

- Event updates, changes or cancellations can be posted immediately to keep all volunteers informed up to and through the day of the event.

- Volunteer activity feedback, kudos and event success details can be added, bringing extra value to your volunteerism activities.

- And finally, a blog can be an archive of your volunteerism activities. Have volunteer coordinators and volunteers post their how-to for creating a particular event and to provide feedback for future positive changes to the event.

Free Sites To Host Your Blog

Use one of these blog hosting sites to start your free volunteer blog today:

✓ www.blogger.com
✓ www.wordpress.com
✓ www.weebly.com

49. Online Quilt Auction Utilizes Volunteer Expertise

Hosting an online auction requires significant volunteer support. Just ask officials with the Ovarian Cancer Awareness Quilt Project for the University of Texas M. D. Anderson Cancer Center (Houston, TX), a first-ever event that featured 68 quilts and raised $11,440 for the center's Blanton-Davis Ovarian Cancer Research Program.

The center's department of oncology coordinated the auction, using more than 25 volunteers, says Pamela Weems, program director for community relations in the department of gynecologic oncology. She notes that many of the volunteers "were M. D. Anderson employees who like to give back and give from the heart."

To locate volunteers in your organization and community and appropriately assign them to help with an online quilt auction, Weems says:

❑ Appoint volunteers with quilting knowledge to the planning committee and to display the quilts.

❑ Have volunteers with photography expertise take pictures of quilts and those volunteers with a love of scrapbooking create a memory book of each year's event.

❑ Assign Web-savvy volunteers or staff to create a website page dedicated to the online auction.

❑ Have volunteers monitor the quilt displays at your organization, acting also as docents and wearing white gloves to protect the quilts from public handling. Create fact cards about each quilt that are available to the volunteers and to the public.

❑ Have volunteers staff quilt festival booths and distribute information about your event to create a buzz within the quilting community.

❑ Have quilting volunteers host a sew-in to support quilters assembling and building quilts and to provide print materials on the cause for which you are raising funds.

❑ Ask quilting experts to help you determine the value of each quilt.

Source: Pamela Weems, Program Director for Community Relations in the Department of Gynecologic Oncology at The University of Texas M. D. Anderson Cancer Center, Houston, TX. Phone (713) 792-2765.
E-mail: gynonccommunityrelations@mdanderson.org

50. Communicate With Teens in Language They Understand

For persons who do not fall into the age range of 13 to 19, teenagers may seem like they come from a different planet. Communicating with teens as a volunteer manager can seem daunting as you wonder if your message is having an impact.

To help guarantee your important information gets to your young volunteers, speak their language. Use one or all of these teen-friendly techniques to get your message across:

✓ **Facebook.** Set up a Facebook page at www.facebook.com specifically for your teen volunteers. Use this free online social network to post volunteer-relevant topics, sched-

ules and events. Volunteers who sign up as fans of the page will receive automatic notification when content is updated.

✓ **Internet presence.** Create a Web page specifically geared to teen volunteers. Add a page to your current website that makes announcements and includes updates for your teen volunteers, along with volunteer activities, group schedules and kudos for teens who deserve a pat on the back.

51. Online Recruitment Tip: Who is info@yourwebsite.com?

Millions of people use the Internet every day and some of them are coming to your website for information on volunteering. Don't run the risk of turning them away by not including your contact information on your site.

Avoid using a generic contact, such as info@ yourwebsite.com. Instead, list the name, phone number and

e-mail address of the volunteer manager or the name of someone at your organization that people can call or e-mail directly. In today's fast-paced, Internet world, impersonal contact contributes to the decline of good customer service — don't let it do so in your organization.

52. Online Calendars Ease Volunteer Scheduling

Look into adding or updating your online calendar to make it work for your volunteer management duties as well as for your volunteers themselves.

Online calendars can help you plan special events, volunteer trainings and meetings or just keep everyone apprised of their volunteer schedules by providing real-time updates and 24-hour access.

The online tools, which are often free, offer the ability to link to an existing website as well as send e-mail reminders or text messages to numerous contacts.

Check Out Online Calendars

Check these sites for an online calendar that best fits your unique needs:

- Time and Date (www.timeanddate.com/calendar/)
- Google (www.google.com/calendar)
- Bravenet (www.bravenet.com/webtools/calendar/)
- Cozi (www.cozi.com)
- Yahoo! (www.calendar.yahoo.com)
- WORKetc (www.worketc.com)

53. Online Friend Groups Gain Volunteer Attention

Employing the latest online options to connect people with your cause is an important component of nurturing the volunteers of today and tomorrow.

At UC Santa Cruz (UCSC) of Santa Cruz, CA, staff devote a website page exclusively highlighting opportunities for students, staff, faculty and community members to get involved through service, both on and off campus.

The effort is paying off. In 2008 alone, UCSC students, staff and faculty contributed an estimated 1 million volunteer hours to schools and other nonprofits in Santa Cruz County. Nearly one-third of UCSC's 15,278 students volunteer or participate in unpaid internships each school year.

Listed on the site's Volunteer Opportunities page (www.ucsc.edu/alumni_friends/volunteer.asp) are 14 specific groups offering volunteer activities called Friends Groups and five other programs (UC Santa Cruz Alumni Association, UC Santa Cruz Foundation, Admission Outreach Volunteers Programs, Career Advice Network and Legislative Advocacy Network).

Friends Groups — comprising community members, staff, faculty and students — are officially recognized campus support groups. Members of the groups are generally considered donors to the campus for the service they provide. These include the Arboretum Associates, Friends of the UCSC Library, Friends of the Farm and Garden, and the Women's Club.

"UC Santa Cruz is very fortunate to have hundreds of friends and volunteers who generously give of their time, energy and resources that contribute to the educational experience on campus," says Liz Evanovich, community relations coordinator. "Our volunteers often mention the satisfaction that comes from being part of the life of a research university and the feeling of being personally enriched by their contributions.

"Internships are an integral part of many programs and majors on campus but not a requirement per se of all of them," says Evanovich. "The internships give students real-world experience in conjunction with their studies."

Source: Liz Evanovich, Community Relations Coordinator, UC Santa Cruz, Santa Cruz, CA. Phone (831) 459-1325. E-mail: lize@ucsc.edu

54. Include Volunteer Descriptions on Your Website

You already know it's wise to develop job descriptions for volunteer positions. They help would-be volunteers know exactly what's expected of them.

Why not post descriptions on the volunteer segment of your website?

Officials with the Nashville Ronald McDonald House (Nashville, TN) offer descriptions for both family and group volunteers at www.rmhnashville.com/volunteer/index.html.

The PDF-format descriptions spell out scheduling shifts, age requirement, term commitment, training expectations, medical requirements, background check requirements and more.

For more info: Nashville Ronald McDonald House Charities of Nashville, Nashville, TN. Phone (615) 343-4000. E-mail: volunteer@rmhnashville.com

55. Online Volunteer Database Benefits Community, Nonprofits

Instead of nonprofits competing with one another to recruit volunteers, encourage your nonprofit to take the lead and establish a central location where nonprofits in your community or region can post volunteer positions and people in the community can learn of those positions.

Nonprofit organizations in Rochester, MN, have benefited from doing so since 1982.

Jeff Ballew, volunteer and community engagement specialist, United Way of Olmsted County (Rochester, MN), says 150 agencies currently volunteer opportunities on Volunteer Solutions, an online database powered by United eWay. Ballew says the database originated in the community's volunteer center but became a part of the United Way of Olmsted County's efforts when the two organizations merged in 2004.

"Often people who are interested in volunteering don't know whom to call," he says. "This online resource gives those people one central place to visit to find out that information and other resources they may not have considered."

The database offers an array of opportunities, from single-day projects to ongoing projects to volunteering for an event that may take a few days or several weeks.

Visitors to the site are not required to register but have the opportunity to do so when first visiting the site. By selecting a user name and password the prospective volunteer can conduct a narrow search by identifying keywords, selecting a city, ZIP code, a certain area or a specific opportunity.

For a broader search, volunteers can elect to identify interests with specific categories. Following is a sample of options volunteers will see when they visit the site:

Community Interest

- Building Skills for Self-sufficiency
- Nurturing Children and Youth
- Harvest for the Hungry
- Community Basics
- Promoting Health

With which social group(s) would you like to work?

- Agency only
- Infants/Preschoolers
- Disaster Victims
- Law Offenders
- Minorities
- Animal Related
- Disabled
- Low-income/ Poverty
- Religious Groups

I am interested in opportunities available to:

- Adults (55-plus)
- Court-appointed
- Group Size (11-15)
- Families
- Service-learning
- Summer Youth Volunteers

Which categories best describe your interests:

- Arts and Culture
- Environment
- Special Event Support
- Healthcare
- Technology
- Communication and Marketing

Statistics Illustrate Database Success

Jeff Ballew, volunteer and community engagement specialist, United Way of Olmsted County (Rochester, MN), shares some statistics regarding the community's Volunteer Solutions Database, in place since 1982:

- On average the database receives 100 hits a month
- In 2007, more than 1,000 new people registered on the site to look for volunteer opportunities
- More than 3,000 people are registered in the system
- The database is free to participating nonprofits and volunteers

---

Ballew says the database is marketed in several ways including the organization's website, area media outlets (e.g., newspaper, local TV and radio), sharing the resource with each year's Leadership Greater Rochester class, through a link on a local TV news station's website and via a monthly spotlight on a noon news broadcast.

Source: Jeff Ballew, Volunteer and Community Engagement Specialist, United Way of Olmsted County, Rochester, MN. Phone (507) 287-2002. E-mail: jeffb@uwolmsted.org

56. Get More Mileage From Your Website

Logging the hours of off-site volunteers usually requires a lot of paperwork, including the signature of the volunteer's immediate supervisor. Elaine Hanson, director, RSVP, Waldorf College (Forest City, IA), felt the process was condescending for adult volunteers.

The college's webmaster and IT department explained she could integrate an online posting system to her existing website. Now, each volunteer supervisor receives a pin number and can log their volunteer's hours in from any location.

Hanson says the information is kept in an account that is saved on the server. A volunteer or student helps download and record the hours. An update is done every fall to add or change pin numbers. The online tracking also meets all of her federal guidelines.

If your organization does not have a webmaster or IT department, ask your local college or university if students are available for a Web internship or ask a local computer business to assist.

Source: Elaine Hanson, Director, RSVP, Waldorf College, Forest City, IA. Phone (641) 585-8294. E-mail: hansone@waldorf.edu

57. Web Tool Boosts Online Recruitment

Think of it as a charity-focused Monster.com, combined with the scope of Craigslist, powered by a sophisticated search engine and personal customer service.

Bintro.com (New York, NY), a free website that matches individuals to job openings, business opportunities and non-profits nationwide, relaunched in April 2010. The relaunch makes use of the latest semantics technology, says Richard Stanton, CEO, "which allows the website to draw a relationship between two people who make different statements, but want to get to the same end goal."

"For example, someone may say that he is looking for a group that focuses on 'environmental causes.'" Stanton explains. "Meanwhile, a charitable organization may describe itself as being dedicated to the promotion of 'green energy.' Semantic data allows us to recognize that a relationship exists between the keywords."

Officials with Grassroots.org (New York, NY), which provides other nonprofits nationwide with free technologies and resources to boost efficiency and productivity, used Bintro.com in 2009 to bring on new volunteers. A request using the tool asking for volunteers in Web design and graphic design brought 55 leads.

"Bintro is a wonderful tool for nonprofit organizations in need of skilled volunteers," says Laura Benack, Grassroots. org interim executive director. Previously, Grassroots.org relied solely on Craigslist posts for volunteer recruitment, Benack says. "Bintro has helped us immensely by referring talented, skilled volunteers directly to our organization."

She gives Bintro.com high marks for customer service, too.

"Bintro's uniqueness lies in the personalized attention that each nonprofit receives," Benack says. "When we recommended Bintro to our members, 38 of them contacted Bintro, and each was guided through the process of finding volunteers by a Bintro team member."

Sources: Laura Benack, Interim Executive Director, Grassroots.org, New York, NY. Phone (800) 252-0015. E-mail: laura@grassroots.org. Website: www.grassroots.org
Richard Stanton, Chief Executive Officer, Bintro.com, Hoboken, NJ. Phone (646) 736-0393. E-mail: rstanton@bintro.com. Website: www.bintro.com

58. Blogging Made Simple

Have you considered posting a personal or professional blog (online journal)?

Large volunteer organizations, such as Charity Channel and World Volunteer Web, have turned to blogging as a resource and communication tool.

If you have considered this latest communication trend but are unsure of where to start, there are avenues volunteer managers can use to launch a blog.

Certain websites offer free start up for people on a restricted budget. For example, www.blogger.com allows you to create a blog in three steps: 1) create an account, 2) name your blog, and 3) choose a template.

Websites also offer upgrades as an option to new clients with an annual fee. Some upgrades may include: topic categories, keyword searching, comments and funds solicitation.

Other websites, such as JournalSpace, Movable Type and Livejournal, are additional tools that enable individuals to create blogs.

Blogging, an instant interactive form of communication, allows people to share and gather information from business professionals and friends.

59. Link to Social Media Networks

In today's technologically savvy world, tweeting isn't just for the birds.

Even members of Congress use social media like Twitter.com to stay in touch with constituents in real time, sending brief text messages, "tweeting", that can be viewed on the Internet, cell phones and on other portable communications devices.

Facebook (www.facebook.com), LinkedIn (www.linkedin.com), Flickr (www.flickr.com) and YouTube (www.youtube.com) are just a few of the free online social media sites where you can create an account or group to communicate with existing volunteers and recruit new ones.

To put these social networking tools to use promoting your special event, increase your organization's online presence and boost awareness of your mission:

❑ **Launch a photo album and blog on Flickr.** Some of your volunteers have traveled to Africa on behalf of your organization. Start an account where they can post photos, write about their activities and share links to news with those at home.

❑ **Start a Facebook group about your event.** Once you have recruited or identified supporters who already use Facebook, you can send invitations to meetings, post photo albums, give daily progress reports about completed tasks and reservations and advertise jobs that still need to be done.

❑ **Twitter messages to spread news.** Your committee meeting has been canceled, but you can't call everyone in time. Twitter allows you to log on to your account and spread the word to many users at once, who can in turn notify others of the change in plans.

❑ **Study social media options for the best fit.** Chances are that many of your volunteers already have accounts on LinkedIn, Twitter, Facebook, YouTube or Flickr. Most of these sites link to each other, so news you share can have a positive ripple effect. Portal websites, like www.socialmediaanswers.com, give tutorials on how to build and cultivate your own network and describe the benefits of the most popular and versatile services.

60. Online Training Streamlines Orientation Process

Switching from a traditional volunteer orientation in a classroom setting to an online format could save your organization time and money.

Beth Upham, manager of volunteer services at Morristown Memorial Hospital (Morristown, NJ), has made that switch with superior results.

Upham's standard training process required her to train several adult learners over the course of many evenings — a time-consuming task. At Morristown Memorial Hospital, assistance from nearly 200 volunteers is needed each day within the eight-building system. Upham trains nearly 300 volunteers each year to keep the volunteer forces strong. With so many volunteers, she says, training in a traditional way was no longer fitting the bill.

"It was cumbersome, some people couldn't make it, and it became a real problem," says Upham about her traditional training method.

Using Moodle.org — a free Web application that educators can use to create effective online learning sites — Upham was able to easily develop an online learning component that gives volunteers the flexibility to train at their own pace onsite without the need of a formalized training session. The process reinforces volunteer learning and can be done the same day volunteer applicants take tuberculosis tests or while waiting for results of their criminal background checks.

Upham developed online training in a 40-question, open-book testing format, which eliminates the need for evening training sessions in a classroom setting. Volunteers may take the test seven days a week from 8:30 a.m. to 5 p.m. at the hospital when it fits their personal schedules.

"Volunteers are saving gas, saving time and they're learning so much more with more freedom," says Upham. "The length of time for onboarding our volunteers has dramatically decreased with online training."

To find out more about Moodle's course management system, go to www.moodle.org.

Source: Beth Upham, Manager of Volunteer Services and Pastoral Care, Morristown Memorial Hospital, Morristown, NJ.
Phone (973) 971-5476. E-mail: Beth.Upham@atlantichealth.org.
Website: www.morristownmemorialhospital.org

61. Top 10 List Emphasizes Volunteer Needs

The importance of a Top 10 list isn't only significant for David Letterman and his faithful viewers. The Red Door Animal Shelter (Chicago, IL) has found that a Top 10 list of volunteer opportunities is a simple yet effective way to express their current volunteer needs.

At the Red Door website, volunteers can easily locate the organization's top ten critical needs from volunteers. The importance of this Top 10 list for Red Door includes help with laundry, driving, shelter shopping, animal caretaking, foster homes, veterinary technicians, phone calls, adoptions, special events and special projects.

Matt Gannon, manager of Red Door, explains why this top ten list has become so important to this nonprofit:

- It was important for us to highlight our volunteer needs because both volunteers and prospective volunteers like to know what opportunities they can choose to make a difference with our organization. So, even if someone says "Well, I'm not really a cat person (or dog person, etc.)," they can look at the list of needs and say, "but, I would be more than willing to help with transporting animals, or to come in and do laundry for a day or some other listed task."

- Volunteers enjoy having the list – which of course, is not all inclusive of opportunities available – to refer to from time to time. As an organization, we leave it up to volunteers to decide the areas and ways that they are comfortable helping out with. Some volunteers only do socialization with animals, some only help with fundraising and events. This way, volunteers can define specialties they excel in, as opposed to being assigned volunteer work they may not feel comfortable doing.

- The top 10 list has helped both with recruitment as it allows prospective volunteers to stop by and say "what do you need from me?" and it helps with retention as some volunteers who may be feeling some burn out from working in one particular area, can find other ways to support the shelter.

Consider creating your own "Top 10" list to effectively manage volunteer opportunities within your organization.

Source: Matt Gannon, Manager, Red Door Animal Shelter, Chicago, IL. Phone (773) 764-2242. E-mail: mgannon@reddoorshelter.org. Website: www.reddoorshelter.org

62. Pros and Cons of Publishing an E-newsletter

Almost all volunteers, young and old, will have access to the Internet and an e-mail address. Consider e-newsletters (created on the computer and sent out via e-mail) to keep your volunteers informed and updated.

Anne Taylor, volunteer coordinator, Make-A-Wish Foundation of the Mid-South (Memphis, TN), has used e-publications for the last six years. She offers pros and cons to putting the volunteer newsletter in this format.

Pro's:

- There are virtually no printing or mailing costs.
- The newsletters are easy to format.
- Since there is no printing or mailing time, the newsletters can go out weekly, keeping volunteers engaged and informed.
- There is a decreased need for volunteer support (e.g., folding or sorting for mailing).
- For volunteers who don't have e-mail (about 25 percent of Taylor's audience), a printed copy can be sent by snail mail.

Con's:

- Taylor often has to dig for information to fill the weekly e-newsletters.
- Technical issues can arise that affect your internal computer system or your online server. For example, sending mass e-mails makes your computer system more susceptible to spam e-mails and viruses.
- Distribution methods could affect readership. Taylor says e-mail merge worked great because she could change the subject line to reflect each newsletter, thus piquing interest. But, because of technical issues, the foundation found it necessary to use an outside company to deliver the e-newsletters. When sent by a third party, the subject lines are generic. Taylor says only 30 percent of her intended audience reads the e-newsletter. She believes that readers are more likely to disregard e-mails with generic headings.

Source: Anne Taylor, Volunteer Coordinator, Make-A-Wish Foundation of the Mid-South, Memphis, TN. Phone (901) 692-9511. E-mail: ataylor@midsouth.wish.org

63. Use Website to Showcase Your Faculty, Staff, Volunteers

Showcase the people who make your organization strong with an online section dedicated to highlighting members of your staff, key volunteers or contributors.

Communications staff at McDaniel College (Westminster, MD) call their online spotlight "Hill People." Launched in 2005, the Hill People section features a faculty member's photo and a brief statement regarding his/her expertise. Currently, features on six faculty members appear on a rotating basis.

According to Joyce Muller, associate vice president, communications and marketing, the feature's purpose is to "highlight faculty who are experts in their fields. Visitors can contact us or use the search function to learn more.

"We identify who is both newsworthy and media-friendly" in choosing persons for the spotlight, says Muller. Faculty members are asked in person or by phone about being included. A communications team member takes the person's photo with a digital camera and writes the short statement accompanying the photo.

The communications team (three staff members including Muller) spends minimal time updating this section and no major costs are involved, she says. They write the features in Microsoft Word and upload them into the content management system. The template automatically distributes the information and puts each faculty feature into rotation, appearing on various pages of the organization's website.

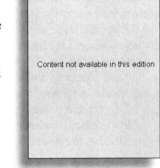

Content not available in this edition

Muller shares this advice with other organizations thinking of creating a similar feature, saying, "Think content first, graphics second, and keep it short."

Source: Joyce Muller, Associate Vice President, Communications and Marketing, McDaniel College, Westminster, MD. Phone (410) 857-2292. Website: www.mcdaniel.edu

64. New Website Offers Insight on Volunteering Trends

A new government-sponsored website, www.Volunteering InAmerica.gov, offers a comprehensive look at volunteering trends in the United States. The site includes a breakdown on trends and highlights by state as well as major cities.

A report recently featured on the website details volunteering trends as identified by the Corporation for National and Community Service. Created by Congress in 1993, the CNCS (www.cncs.org) is a public-private partnership that oversees three national service initiatives: AmeriCorps, Learn and Serve America, and the National Senior Service Corps.

According to the CNCS report, nearly 61 million Americans volunteered in their communities in 2007, giving 8.1 billion hours of service worth $158 billion-plus.

The report's findings also show:

✓ **Voluntourism is strong.** The report includes an analysis of this emerging phenomenon in which volunteers travel out of state to aid in volunteer efforts. In 2007, more than 3.7 million Americans volunteered more than 120 miles from home.

✓ **The volunteering sector is a leaky bucket.** The report underscored the continuing challenge of volunteer retention, with more than one in three American volunteers dropping out between 2006 and 2007. This points to how important it is to give meaningful assignments and use best practices in volunteer management.

✓ **Intensive volunteering is on the rise.** The percentage of volunteers giving more than 100 hours of service a year reached its highest level since 2002, with 35.6 percent of all volunteers contributing at this intensive level.

✓ **College towns are volunteering hot spots.** The high rankings of college towns like Iowa City, IA, and Madison, WI, reflect the known positive correlation between higher levels of education and volunteering.

✓ **Women volunteer more than men, and working mothers have the highest volunteer rate.** About 29.3 percent of women volunteered in 2007, compared to 22.9 percent of men. Women with children and women who work also have higher volunteer rates.

65. Target Website Helps Train, Recruit, Retain Volunteers

Your organization's website may be the first contact many potential volunteers have with your nonprofit. Make sure it is not their last by offering detailed information about your volunteer opportunities.

"I think it's important for volunteers to know exactly what the various positions entail before they sign on to assist," says Karen Neely Faryniak, associate vice president for college relations, Dickinson College (Carlisle, PA). "Otherwise, we're setting them and us up for failure."

To help website visitors understand what is involved with volunteering for the college, staff created the Dickinson Volunteer Network — a subsite dedicated solely to providing prospective and existing volunteers with timely, useful information.

Part of the college's general website, the site (www. dickinson.edu/volunteer/development.html) entices visitors with the welcoming words: "Browse through the menu at the top of the page to learn why you should volunteer and what's new at Dickinson. The menu on the left will direct you to specific volunteer areas."

Clicks on those links lead visitors to full volunteer job descriptions for each opportunity, volunteer testimonials, ongoing training opportunities, contact information and video messages from President William G. Durden.

The site's job descriptions page is its website's fourth most-visited page, following only the main page, the admissions page and the page that lists all of the volunteer opportunities. Faryniak says this rank illustrates that alumni are taking their prospective volunteer roles seriously, fully checking out the responsibilities of the positions before committing to them.

Video training modules on the site serve as primary training tools for some volunteer roles, which Faryniak says saves time and money over other methods.

One adjustment made on the site has been to make staff contact information easily accessible up front, says Faryniak, noting that doing so alleviates frustration and the potential loss of a volunteer.

The college currently has approximately 2,500 volunteers.

Source: Karen Neely Faryniak, Associate Vice President for College Relations, Dickinson College, Carlisle, PA. Phone (717) 245-1578. E-mail: faryniak@dickinson.edu

66. Should You Start a Blog?

Considering creating a blog?

"A blog is a more informal way of giving visitors a behind-the-scenes update to what's going on in your organization," says Craig Richetti, webmaster, Alex's Lemonade Stand Foundation (Wynnewood, PA), a nonprofit devoted to fighting childhood cancer. "It creates a medium where visitors can add their comments and insights, allowing their voice to not only be heard by the organization, but by everyone who reads the blog."

Blogs are easy to use and manage, and can often be created free through various services, Richetti says.

The webmaster answers additional questions about websites and blogs:

What is the fundamental difference between a blog and a website?

"A website is typically a place for news, information and a host for organization resources. A blog offers a dynamic portal for conversation between the blogger and the reader."

What are the benefits to having both?

"Your website will offer organization details such as contact information and the history behind your organization. A blog offers a personal touch for updates about event details while allowing a reader to comment on a submission, making it a powerful communication tool."

What advice would you give organizations that have both a blog and website?

"On the main page of your website, post a link to your blog and vice versa. This way, visitors have easy access to both the blog where they can contribute comments, and your website where they'll find out more about your organization. A blog offers the ability to add features more easily than a website. Administrators can add RSS feeds, which are tools used to obtain headlines from favorite websites.

"You may find it easier to update your blog daily since multiple people in an organization have the ability to contribute to it, whereas updating a website is a more involved process. Websites are updated when there is new information about your organization, or if you have a significant change to the organization."

Source: Craig Richetti, Webmaster, Alex's Lemonade Stand Foundation, Wynnewood, PA. Phone (610) 649-3034. E-mail: craig@alexslemonade.com

67. Keep Virtual Volunteers Close

Macdonald Youth Services (MYS) of Winnipeg, Manitoba, Canada is a youth-focused organization that manages virtual volunteers.

While the organization's virtual volunteers once held tutoring and teaching roles, their virtual volunteer base has expanded to include a variety of roles including video production, updating the human resources portion of the MYS website, and assisting with the creation of brochures and posters.

Sean Crawford, manager of external relations, offers tips for communicating closely with virtual volunteers:

❑ Stay in touch with virtual volunteers, even when they're not actively involved in a current project. At MYS, the external relations and human resources staff are in regular contact with active volunteers to make them aware of upcoming projects or to see how an existing project is progressing.

❑ Send lists of upcoming projects to virtual volunteers to gain interest in projects. MYS recently sent out such a list and scored multiple poster designs from available virtual volunteers, giving the planning committee multiple options from which to choose.

❑ Offer virtual volunteers recognition as you would other volunteers. At MYS, virtual volunteers are recognized at the annual staff appreciation event and are sent small tokens of appreciation. Recently, all virtual volunteers received a flash drive.

Source: Sean Crawford, Manager of External Relations, Macdonald Youth Services, Winnipeg, Manitoba, Canada. Phone (204) 477-1722. E-mail: sean.crawford@mys.mb.ca

68. Online Resources Educate Current, Potential Volunteers

With a quick visit to the hospital website, volunteers and potential volunteers at La Rabida Children's Hospital (Chicago, IL) can find answers to frequently asked questions, or FAQs, about the volunteer system.

Clicking the volunteer tab at the hospital's main Web page and scrolling down to the header FAQs, website visitors find a wealth of information about the volunteer process at La Rabida, from age restrictions to volunteer expectations.

"We added FAQs for two reasons," says Judi Blake-more, manager of volunteer services: "Transparency so that everyone has the same information, and so that applicants are more knowledgeable from the beginning of the process."

Consider adding a similar component to your website and volunteer brochure to educate people on how the volunteer process works at your organization.

Source: Judi Blakemore, Manager of Volunteer Services, La Rabida Children's Hospital, Chicago, IL. Phone (773) 256-5985. E-mail: jblakemore@larabida.org. Website: www.larabida.org

69. Encourage Your Volunteers to Form an Online Chat Group

Looking to connect your volunteers and possibly attract younger persons to your volunteer ranks? Consider establishing an online chat group.

Online chat groups are free and easy to set up. Many of the main search engines, like Yahoo.com, offer this service.

Kathy Cahill, volunteer services coordinator, Lee County Parks and Recreation (Fort Myers, FL), says one of her groups of volunteers established and maintains an online chat group specifically for its location. The group is a great way for the volunteers to recruit and stay connected, she says.

While the group is completely volunteer-run, Cahill did set some guidelines with the volunteers to make sure the content was appropriate. All content must be related to volunteers and/or wetland conservation.

Source: Kathy Cahill, Volunteer Services Coordinator, Lee County Parks and Recreation, Fort Myers, FL. Phone (239) 432-2159. E-mail: kcahill@leegov.com

70. Showcase Volunteer Opportunities With Online Slide Show

Enticing potential volunteers with an online slide show of opportunities has helped St. Jude Children's Research Hospital (Memphis, TN) recruit volunteers for two years.

"It is a terrific, visual way for volunteers to learn more about our volunteer opportunities," says Kathryn Berry Carter, director of volunteer services. "Our slide show includes pictures of volunteers in action, a brief description of our available volunteer opportunities and requirements for each position."

She recommends the following tips for creating an online slide show:

- Take photos of volunteers in action as often as you can. Each of the 12 opportunities featured on the site rotate among multiple pictures. "The photos provide ... a mental picture of what the volunteer experience will be like," Berry Carter says. "They can visually see and imagine themselves participating as a volunteer."

- Think about your volunteer opportunities from the volunteers' perspective. What might interest them?

- Do not hesitate to include requirements. "Volunteers need to know what they are getting into and the expectations," Berry Carter explains.

- Keep the postings accurate and up-to-date.

St. Jude typically receives 30 volunteer applications each month. Although there is no way to determine a direct link between the slide show and the number of applications, Berry Carter says roughly half are online submissions, thereby indicating a likelihood of having viewed the slide show.

Source: Kathryn Berry Carter, Director of Volunteer Services, St. Jude Children's Research Hospital, Memphis, TN. Phone (901) 495-2277. E-mail: kathryn.berry-carter@stjude.org. Website: www.stjude.org

An online slide show for St. Jude Children's Research Hospital (Memphis, TN) features photos and descriptions of volunteering opportunities. (Screenshot photo by Laura Hajaar.)

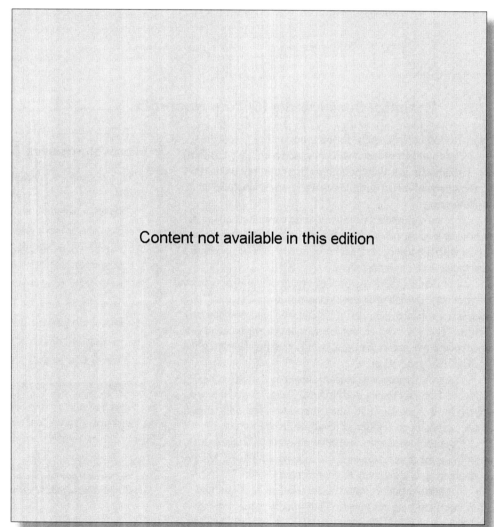

Content not available in this edition

71. Create a Landing Page When Making Changes to Your Website

When staff at Bates College created a new format and new distribution system for BatesNews — a quick scan for busy people, with links to more information — they wanted to ensure that people followed. Director of Communications and Media Relations Bryan McNulty says they did this with the creation of a landing page that allows people to easily move from the old legacy e-newsletter to the new format. Here's how it works:

For the last two issues of the legacy e-newsletter, the following message ran at the top of the page, inside a yellow banner: "BatesNews, the monthly update created for alumni, parents and friends of Bates, is moving to a new format and using a new distribution system. BatesNews was created as and will remain a quick scan for busy people, with links to more information. To continue receiving BatesNews, you will need to opt-in here."

The opt-in here link takes visitors to the landing page (http://home.bates.edu/elements/subscribe-batesnews/), where they connect with the college's publications and any of their social media accounts. McNulty says the landing page not only bumped up the number of monthly digest subscribers, but daily, weekly and by topic subscribers as well.

Source: Bryan McNulty, Director of Communications and Media Relations, Bates College, Lewiston, ME. Phone (207) 786-6330. E-mail: bmcnulty@bates.edu.

72. Maximize Social Media for Your Nonprofit

Is microvolunteering right for your nonprofit?

The founders of Urbantastic (Vancouver, Canada) think so. Urbantastic is a Web portal that promotes nonprofits that embrace social media and furthers the trend to include microvolunteering.

A microvolunteer is someone who completes tasks, in whole or in part, offsite from the organization being assisted, often with the use of an Internet-connected device such as a computer, PDA or smartphone.

"Put plainly, there is a pool of young, talented people who are not actively donating time to causes they believe in," says Benjamin Johnson, founder of Urbantastic along with Heath Johns. "There is a desire, but the avenues of engagement are inadequate. We are in the process of correcting this using the tools of that generation.

"Microvolunteering, in many ways, is the difference between Barack Obama and Howard Dean," says Johnson. "Both built legions of dedicated supporters, but only Barack built legions upon legions of small-scale supporters.

"Nonprofits need to continue to find new blood to support them, be it as future staff, donors or volunteers. Microvolunteering is a gateway to greater involvement."

To recruit microvolunteers, Johnson says, "Go where they are. Don't expect them to visit your website. Post no-

tices on Craigslist (www.craigslist.com), create a fan page on Facebook (www.facebook.com) or post opportunities on Twitter (www.twitter.com)."

Source: Heath Johns and Benjamin Johnson, Founders, Urbantastic, Vancouver, Canada. Phone (778) 990-4977. E-mail: ben@urbantastic.com

Microvolunteering Tasks

What tasks can microvolunteers do to benefit your nonprofit?

- Tweet on Twitter (www.twitter.com) about events.
- Start a blog about your nonprofit's events and programs.
- Recruit volunteers via Facebook (www.facebook.com) or e-mail.
- Research a song for a photo slideshow.
- Select book bags for a children's program.
- Distribute posters around the community.
- Photograph directors or volunteers for the website.
- Translate a website's home page into another language.

73. Caring for Virtual Volunteers

Virtual volunteers need special care. Two volunteer managers offer insight into nurturing these off-site volunteers:

"It is important to maintain regular communication with virtual volunteers, such as a biweekly or monthly e-mail. Virtual volunteers also need to be able to contact you via e-mail or phone and receive a response fairly quickly to answer any questions they may have about their project. Letting virtual volunteers know about the progress of a project and how much their work is appreciated is also important, since they oftentimes cannot see the overall progression or accomplishments of a project from home."

— *Autumn Gonzalez, Volunteer Coordinator, Indiana State Library (Indianapolis, IN)*

"The volunteer manager should make sure that they are keeping in constant communication with the virtual volunteers to make sure projects are getting completed and done well in a timely manner. A more technological approach should be used, utilizing the Internet, telephone and Web cams for update meetings. Set up a volunteer link or forum through which local and virtual volunteers can share ideas and get to know each other. Encourage local volunteers to communicate with the virtual volunteers so that they, too, feel like part of the family. A skilled, passionate, reliable, motivated, dedicated and self-disciplined virtual volunteer is a blessing. Be sure to thank these people often."

— *Rachel Thuermer, Program Director, Dare to Dream Theatre, Inc. (Manitowoc, WI)*

74. Website Features Corporate Partnerships

The American Red Cross in Greater New York values its corporate partnerships. So much so, they've devoted a page to that specific volunteer opportunity at the www.nyredcross.org website.

Three specific corporate partnerships opportunities that local supporting companies can do to contribute significantly to this Red Cross include:

- Philanthropy
- Volunteerism
- Preparedness Training

According to David Gibbs, director of corporate and foundation relations, the corporate partnership page is designed to introduce volunteerism with the Red Cross as a viable community service experience for company employees. Additionally, the page alerts casual website visitors that the Red Cross is interested in company participation beyond philanthropy and contributions by detailing hands-on opportunities that exist.

Through corporate partnership, the Red Cross of Greater New York has trained nearly 40 corporate teams of Ready When the Time Comes (RWTC) reserve disaster volunteers.

The RWTC preparedness training is the cornerstone corporate volunteer opportunity featured on the corporate partnerships page, which provies a description of the program, services provided by RWTC volunteers and requirements of the program.

The participating RWTC Corporate Partners are listed on this Web page to not only offer validity to corporate giving by showing who is involved and trained in the program, but also to offer recognition to participating RWTC companies.

"Corporate relations have evolved to a higher level of engagement where partnerships are related with key issues such as volunteerism," says David Gibbs, director of corporate and foundation relations. "It is our hope that as disaster preparedness and response continues to evolve in Greater New York, the opportunity for American Red Cross in Greater New York to provide meaningful connections for companies will too."

Source: David Gibbs, Director of Corporate and Foundation Relations, American Red Cross in Greater New York, New York, NY. Phone (212) 875-2616. E-mail: gibbsd@nyredcross.org. Website: www.nyredcross.org

75. Medical Center Masters Online Volunteer Orientation

To simplify the orientation process for you and your volunteers, offer it online.

Rather than requiring volunteers to sit through a face-to-face orientation session, an online orientation allows them to work at their own pace in a comfortable setting.

Plus, it makes tracking information much easier for your organization.

Volunteer coordinators at the University of Arkansas for Medical Sciences Medical Center (UAMS) of Little Rock, AR, began an online volunteer orientation a year ago.

Andrea Stokes, former volunteer coordinator and creator of the online orientation, says that when a volunteer's application is received electronically, he/she is asked to complete the online orientation. To do so, volunteers:

- Read through an online version of the volunteer manual. It covers topics ranging from safety codes to policies and procedures to the history of UAMS.

- Complete four tests and/or forms relating directly to material studied: HIPAA, confidentiality, safety and a volunteer contract.

- Receive an e-mail thanking them for completing the orientation and directing them to contact the volunteer department to schedule an interview.

"Essentially and ideally, all interested volunteers who have scheduled an interview have already completed their online orientation session and have an idea of the way UAMS operates, its history and its mission," Stokes explains.

To ensure a participant actually completes the orientation, she says:

- A database tracks each component of the orientation session.

- Applicants take tests to fully ensure they have read and understand the material.

- All volunteer applicants must interview with a staff member. During this time, the staff member evaluates the applicant's skill sets.

Source: Andrea Stokes, Clinical Research Promoter, Arkansas Children's Hospital, Little Rock, AR. Phone (501) 364-3309. E-mail: stokesandreac@uams.edu. Website: www.archildrens.org

Create a Successful Volunteer Orientation — Online

Andrea Stokes, former volunteer coordinator, University of Arkansas for Medical Sciences Medical Center (Little Rock, AR), offers the following advice for organizations interested in starting an online orientation process:

1. **Ignore the belief that online orientation only appeals to people in a specific age bracket.** "People from every generation are willing to try this as long as you are patient with your instructions and make your module easy to find and easy to understand," she explains.

2. **Be meticulous when editing your website and orientation module.** Stokes says it is important to create a friendly and welcoming look. Additionally, avoid spelling and grammatical errors.

3. **Be prepared to edit and update.** "There is nothing worse than a website that hasn't been edited in more than a year," Stokes says. "If your uniforms have changed, change your pictures. If your confidentiality statement has been revised, don't forget to revise it in your orientation materials. You don't want to mislead volunteers."

4. **Use lots of guinea pigs.** Stokes recommends going through the materials monthly to make sure everything is working properly and is user-friendly.

5. **Invest in a good database.** "Volunteer tracking is essential to maintaining any volunteer program, especially when you are using an online system that may attract individuals who never become volunteers," Stokes says. "Keep all records and, if you can, track all correspondence you make with potential applicants via e-mail, your website, telephone, etc. It's helpful to have those records when you hear from them again."

76. Hospital Volunteering Page: Clean, Precise

Just as one would expect a hospital to be clean and precise, the George Washington University Hospital's (Washington, D.C.) website offers volunteers a clean and precise volunteering page. On the main page of the volunteering section, would-be volunteers can find easy step-by-step instructions on becoming a volunteer, and they are just a click away from finding volunteer opportunities at GWU.

In the past year, Kristin Urbach, director of customer and volunteer service, has recruited 366 volunteers who have provided 16,000 hours of service. The volunteering page helped serve many of those volunteers as a starting point, guiding them through the volunteering process. Every month, nearly 1,600 Web searchers access the Volunteer page at GWU!

Urbach tells us more about this well-designed page:

The entire appearance of GWU Hospital's volunteering page is so clean and concise. How do you think that benefits would-be volunteers?

Due to the information and appearance on our website, in addition to changing the application process to an online one, we have been able to recruit more candidates.

The getting-started area offering the four steps to becoming a volunteer appears to be an efficient way to communicate with volunteers. When volunteers call in inquiring about opportunities, are they simply directed to the Volunteer page since the steps are outlined so cleanly?

When volunteers call about opportunities, we respond to their questions and also provide them with the website address. When they call us, we want to be able to provide great customer service by thanking them for their interest, responding to their questions and directing them to the website. When they do not reach a live person, the voicemail provides our website address and recommends they review it for information. As a result, we do not receive many calls because the website is informative and user-friendly.

Peruse your volunteering page at your nonprofit's

Content not available in this edition

website and compare it to that of GWU Hospital at www.gwhospital.com/Volunteering to see where you might tweak it for preciseness — the changes could net more volunteers!

Source: Kristin Urbach, Director of Customer and Volunteer Service, Washington, D.C. Phone (202) 715-4188. E-mail: Kristin.urbach@gwu-hospital.com. Website: www.gwhospital.com

77. Website Reveals Detailed Volunteer Descriptions, Graph

Clarify duties, expectations and anticipated time commitments for would-be volunteers to help them choose assignments that best match their interests and abilities.

More than 1,300 persons volunteer through The Friends of Filoli, a nonprofit organization charged with caring for the picturesque country estate, Filoli Center (Woodside, CA). The property is an historic site of the National Trust for Historic Preservation. Visitors enjoy the beauty of the home's architecture of the early 1900s as well as the surrounding Santa Cruz Mountains and 16-acre formal gardens.

To match the most suitable volunteer for an open position, Carol Croce, vice president of volunteer resources, developed a detailed graph of available opportunities.

The graph is broken into subsets of volunteering types and includes a description of the activity, attire necessary, requirements of the volunteer, any prerequisite training, and the level of commitment the assignment involves.

Croce answers our questions about how the graph benefits the volunteer-driven program:

Have the detailed volunteer descriptions actually helped to recruit volunteers to perform that function?

"Yes. The volunteer opportunities chart is posted on the website to educate potential volunteers about each committee before they complete an application for volunteering. They can choose which committees best meet their interests, skills and time commitment.

"The chart is also used as a handout for Filoli's Volunteer Recruitment Open House, held twice a year. The public is invited to attend the open house to learn about volunteering at Filoli. Committee chairs provide brief presentations outlining their committee's activities, time commitments and training requirements. The handout helps the audience follow the presentations. Most people mark up the chart with their questions for the chairs or circle those committees that are their top choices to join. This makes completing the volunteer application much easier for potential volunteers."

Have you gotten positive feedback regarding how your volunteer opportunities are displayed in the chart?

"Yes. People want to know what activities they will do as volunteers and especially, how much time must be committed to their job. The chart presents this very clearly."

How many volunteers do you work with?

"Filoli currently has over 1,300 volunteers working on 15 standing committees. All committees work year round, though some are more active during the high visitor season from April to July. The committee model works well at Filoli, allowing volunteers to work within smaller groups focused on specific projects."

What advice do you have for creating a volunteer opportunities chart?

"Work with your committee chairs to clarify the descriptions for each part of the chart. Keep the chart updated at least yearly so it reflects the correct time commitments and training requirements for each volunteer job listed. Spend time creating a detailed volunteer opportunities chart that not only features your volunteer opportunities, but answers potential questions by volunteers."

Source: Carol Croce, Vice President of Volunteer Resources, Friends of Filoli, Woodside, CA. Phone (650) 364-8300. E-mail: volunteer@filoli.org. Website: www.filoli.org

Shown at left is a sample of how the volunteer opportunities chart looks at Filoli's.

Content not available in this edition

78. Website Ideas

Are you tailoring your website to the needs and interests of your volunteers?

Increasing numbers of nonprofit organizations — Wellesley College, Wellesley, MA (www.wellesley.edu/Resources/volunteer/index.html) — are including a volunteer tools page on their websites that volunteers can turn to for information and support.

79. Tips for Your Website

■ Does your website include photos of volunteers in action? If not, find someone with a digital camera and take a few candid shots of your volunteers at work to post on your organization's website. With each photograph include a caption that highlights some of the perks — both tangible and personal — your volunteers receive from donating their time.

80. Newsworthy Links Feature Volunteers in Action

At Monroe Carell Jr. Children's Hospital at Vanderbilt (Nashville, TN), links to news sources showing volunteers in action can be found at the center's website at www.vanderbiltchildrens.org.

Posting links to news clips featuring your engaged volunteers offers a clearly defined window on participating within your organization.

Jerry Jones, director of media relations, explains the best practices of utilizing news sources at a website:

How do you attract media attention at Children's and who originates the idea?

We use a variety of sources to attract media to Monroe Carell Jr. Children's Hospital at Vanderbilt. Our media team consists of a regional media person, a national media person, a Children's Hospital media person, as well as a PIO in the cancer center and school of nursing. We communicate and work together to pitch stories. Many of the ideas come from us working our beats and talking to the faculty and staff about new research or interesting patient stories.

How does posting the news link to your site work?

It's important to note that we do not post any video to our sites that a television station airs due to copyright issues. We do post a short summary of the story and links to the story on the media outlet website.

How do you select what to post at the hospital's website? What tips can you share?

Once a story airs and we think it contains information that is important from an educational point of view or great human interest, we post a summary and link to the story. The same goes for posting print or Web articles that someone else has done. It's great to draw attention to these, but be sure not to steal the content. Just link to the original content the media outlet posted. Sometimes these links expire, so you'll want to keep postings fresh and new. We also use the headlines to provide an RSS feed (with the appropriate links) out to our social media networks.

Maximize your news coverage by featuring links at your website. Future volunteers could be captivated by what they see.

Source: Jerry Jones, Director of Media Relations, Monroe Carell Jr. Children's Hospital at Vanderbilt, Nashville, TN. Phone (615) 322-4747. E-mail: jerry.jones@Vanderbilt.edu. Website: www.mc.vanderbilt.edu/npa

81. Match Your Domain Name With Your Organization's Name

Having a website domain name that matches your organization's name makes it easier for visitors to find your site.

If your site name has nothing to do with your organization, it will not only be difficult to find in a search, but people will be less likely to take notice of it. Having a domain name that is the same as your organization's name will attract potential donors and volunteers to your site with ease. It will also help solidify name recognition within the community.

Obtaining your domain name is easy. Sites such as www.networksolutions.com/whois/ allow you to search domain names to see if yours is available. Keep in mind that an accurate domain name will help carve out your place on the Web.

82. Online Orientation Prerequisite to Onsite Training

The Northern Colorado American Red Cross Chapter (Fort Collins, CO) has found a fast, effective way to orient volunteers by offering online orientation and using it as a prerequisite to formal training offered onsite.

According to Sarah Bray, volunteer program coordinator, the online orientation is one of the many benefits of being associated with a national organization. Effective tools are orchestrated and developed by the national organization and individual chapters access those tools for online training.

"Our chapter recommends that our volunteers take both online courses before attending our two-hour new volunteer orientation offered at our chapter headquarters where the potential new volunteers hear stories from current volunteers and staff members as they take a walking tour of our facility," says Bray. "We find that the combination of the online orientation and the walking tour helps the potential volunteer learn more about the organization and also gives us the opportunity to meet and visit with the new volunteer before they start their journey as a volunteer."

The online orientation is broken into a series of four audio and slide modules which include the topics: History, Foundations, Key Services and Commitments. In all, the online orientation takes 70 minutes for a volunteer to complete. Offering online orientation not only conserves staff time, but can also offer volunteers a window on the organization, helping them to determine if your organization is right for them. Find this online orientation at www.northerncolorado.redcross.org to get a feel for what an online orientation should include.

Contact your national headquarters today to determine if online orientation or other training tools are readily available to post at your chapter's website. If you're not associated with a national organization, consider creating your own online orientation to present the mission of your nonprofit to interested volunteers.

Source: Sarah Bray, Volunteer Program Coordinator, American Red Cross Northern Colorado Chapter, Fort Collins, CO.
Phone (970) 226-5728. E-mail: brays@CentennialArc.org.
Website: www.northerncolorado.redcross.org

83. Enhance Your Website to Reel in More Volunteers

How effective is your organization's website at attracting volunteers? Does it account for 10, 30 or 50 percent of your new volunteer candidates?

What if you could say 100 percent?

That is what is being accomplished at Sydney Cooper Senior Smiles (Los Angeles, CA), a 100-percent volunteer-run nonprofit organization that provides companionship to the elderly.

"(Potential volunteers) see we're creative, that we take a different approach to volunteering," says Jill Pizitz-Hochstein, executive director.

The organization's website (www.seniorsmiles.org) is interactive and draws surfers in with a cartoon illustrating the need for volunteers, she says. The site gives multiple options to start volunteering by simply clicking a mouse.

Pizitz-Hochstein told webmaster and volunteer Andrew Zaw she wanted the website to be fun, interesting and interactive. Zaw put in a lot of hours to make that happen. He created the website for free, but Senior Smiles does pay for the domain and name.

Zaw spends two to six hours a week on upkeep for the site.

Potential volunteers are drawn to the website by posts on Volunteermatch.org, Craigslist.org, through trainings and flyers. Pizitz-Hochstein emphasizes that it's important to make volunteering as easy as possible.

Senior Smiles has hundreds of seniors waiting for a companion, which emphasizes the importance of making the volunteering experience enjoyable, notes Catherine Kim, volunteer coordinator.

"We believe an organization like ours should be easy to join so as to allow potential volunteers begin their volunteer experience when they are interested," Kim says. "I realized from my personal experiences with other volunteer organizations that the longer an organization takes to contact and/or start the volunteer, the more the potential volunteer loses interest."

Sources: Jill Pizitz-Hochstein, Executive Director and Catherine Kim, Volunteer Coordinator, Sydney Cooper Senior Smiles, Los Angeles, CA. Phone (310) 459-0490.
E-mail: seniorsmiles4u@seniorsmiles.org

84. Convince Others to Create a Link to Your Site

If you can't get everyone to learn about volunteer opportunities by visiting your website, maybe you can attract them by becoming visible on others' websites.

Make an all-out effort to convince businesses and other groups that have websites to include a link to your website. Whether you use direct mail, phone calls, face-to-face visits or a combination of these methods to get the job done, set a new-links goal for yourself along with a deadline date. That way the project will become a priority you can complete and put behind you. After all, once new links are in place, it's just a matter of responding to inquiries that reach your website.

85. Six Ways to Help Volunteers More Easily Navigate Your Website

No matter how good your website content may be, if visitors to your site can't find it, it's of no use to them and of no benefit to you. Here are six ways to help users more easily navigate your website:

1. Keep navigation link titles short but descriptive.

2. Don't include too many links from your main page. If your website contains more than six to seven pages, include the remaining links on secondary pages.

3. Offer a text alternative to pages with lots of graphics.

4. Make sure users can tell, either by a shaded link or a different colored link, whether the link has already been clicked.

5. Create a site map or contents page so users can easily find sought-after info.

6. Keep the main menu visible and accessible on each page so that users can navigate through the main pages of the site from any page they may be reading.

86. Share Message in Virtual World

For a creative way to connect with donors, volunteers and others, create an online world related to your cause.

Members of the Colorado Association of Libraries (CAL), Lakewood, CO, can join an interest group based on the virtual world of Second Life from Linden Lab (San Francisco, CA), an online 3D interactive virtual reality program that allows users to socialize and participate in individual and group activities.

CAL has paid for the land rental and custom building design in the virtual online world, offering free participation to all members. Second Life hosts continuing education classes on how to develop personal avatars and has already hosted several meetings and programs in-world.

The organization is also establishing a presence on Second Life through a virtual library, virtual workshops, conferences and links to websites where members learn more about smart environmental choices.

"The library is not necessarily a place anymore, but an access to information, especially in remote areas," says Jody Howard, association president. "Second Life helps connect members with common interests. It's just another way to use relevant technology to bring people together."

Source: Jody K. Howard, President, Colorado Association of Libraries, Thornton, CO. Phone (303) 859-1242.
E-mail: jodyhoward@comcast.net

87. Four Questions to Ask to Determine Web Content

If you plan to launch a new or redesigned website, an important first step is determining your website's content.

To give web planners a starting point, Dennis Kenny, president, IlluminAge Communication Partners (Seattle, WA), and staff developed a web content and functionality checklist (shown below).

While they originally created the checklist to aid healthcare and aging services providers and associations, Kenny says the checklist can guide Web planning for any nonprofit agency.

"Our checklist is just a convenient jumping-off point," he says. "It probably won't include every possible form of content or functionality you'd like to consider, but it will name most of them and serve as a starting point."

The list names more than 25 features to consider when designing a website.

To aid in your website design or re-design project, Kenny shares four questions to help determine what to include as content and online functionality:

1. **Who is our audience?** Because every organization is different, the Web planner needs to begin with a clear appreciation of whom the website is meant to serve.

2. **How will they use our website?** To help determine what content will be featured on your website, a successful website should be audience-driven. "A successful website is one that responds as directly as possible to what the website's users need, want and value," says Kenny.

3. **Is it in our budget?** While online content and functionality are less expensive than their print and in-person counterparts, they still come with a price. Kenny recommends asking your Web developer for a cost breakdown and the flexibility to include some elements now, and defer others until later. Kenny says it is also important during website design to plan for future growth as the audience's needs and expectations evolve.

4. **Can we keep it current?** Does your organization have the horsepower (e.g., staffing, volunteers, budget) to maintain the content you seek to include? "Better to leave it out," he says, "than to put it in and have it go stale because no one is available to keep it current."

Source: Dennis Kenny, President, IlluminAge Communication Partners, Seattle, WA. Phone (800) 448-5213, ext. 303. E-mail: dennis@illuminAge.com

Content not available in this edition

Website design experts at IlluminAge Communication Partners (Seattle, WA) created this two-page checklist to help determine website content before designing a new website or revamping an existing one.